LEAP
into the mind
of a suicide

NANCY XIA

PAGE PUBLISHING, INC.
New York, NY

First originally published by Page Publishing, Inc. 2016

ISBN 978-1-68348-477-6 (Paperback)
ISBN 978-1-68348-478-3 (Digital)

Printed in the United States of America

Thanks again for the gift of life.

PROLOGUE

1991, China

As the clock was ticking toward midnight, I still had my eyes wildly open. This was another one of those nights. I imagined seeing two gods sitting above the cloud, stroking their long silver beards, and saying, "Mortals shall live no more than one hundred years old, no more than the life of a turtle." The scene changed. I saw myself lying in a coffin and being lowered beyond the surface of the ground. I then saw that black hole in the universe twirling toward me and sucking me into its eternal darkness . . . One thread of thought branched out into another, slaying every will to sleep. My breath quickened and my heart started to drum. A phobic feeling overshadowed me. I was no stranger to that feeling—closer than a friend and more evil than an enemy. I rose from bed, inhaled and exhaled in hunger. I turned to my mother who was resting peacefully beside me. I put my hand on hers. I needed the warmth of living flesh to chase death away.

I looked out the window and whispered to the full moon, "I wish I would never die."

1

April 2003, Toronto

Twenty to midnight, every decent creature was at rest, except me. Lately, sleep had become a luxury I could not afford. I carefully closed my friend's front door and stepped down to my road of no return. The moon was bright and the sky was clear. A setting like so incompatible with what was about to happen.

On that quiet street, my heartbeats were the only sounds in my ears; in that lonely world, my shadow was my only companion. Will I be alone on this road to heaven? Will I go to heaven at all? Oh well, there is no heaven. I never believed in religion. I was brought up in a country that denounces God and all of its alternatives. I was told that religious people are gullible and uneducated. I was taught that I should rely solely on my own strength. Thus, when there was no way I could climb out of this grave on my own, I chose to bury myself.

I entered a much darker avenue after crossing the intersection. The fear of the night overwhelmed me. My thoughts found dangers behind every bush . . . *Will someone jump out from behind the shadows?* But thinking twice, I felt the irony. *I am going to die.* There is nothing that is more frightening than death. I wished that some devil would jump out at that moment, assault me and kill me. This might be my last chance to taste sex before death. And better yet, he might be my only chance of dying as a sorry victim instead of a pathetic suicide. The pain throbbing in my temples urged me to pick up my speed and fully embrace the darkness.

I heard a big noise coming from behind. I turned back and saw a bus. Even though I could see my condo from where I was, I decided to take that bus. As I stepped onto it, the driver blinked really hard as if confirming he wasn't seeing a wandering ghost. I certainly was not the typical passenger at this time of the night, but the four drunken young men on board were. They were slouching in the front seats with their overstretched legs blocking the passageway. Their baggy denims intimidated me. One of them surveyed me from head to toe with his last bit of sobriety. I did not want to go near them. I remained standing beside the front door, continuously feeding the driver's curiosity. He had no idea that he would be the last person to see me alive.

I got off the bus at the next stop. A small plaza was located at that intersection. There was a short cut to my building via the back of the plaza. I used to work as a cashier in the corner supermarket there. Memories flashed back, and I felt like I was walking home after work. Of course, it was the very last shift of my life. As I turned the corner, I immediately saw my building standing firm under the moonlight. Each balcony looked like a springboard hanging in the air, bouncing up and down to allure me. I wish I could go to the very top one and dive like an Olympian. My unit was on the eighth floor; about twenty-five meters above the grave, *this should be high enough.* "Hurry!" someone was commanding me, an extraterrestrial being that intruded into my consciousness not long ago. It had changed me into some sort of automaton. My only program was self-destruction.

Each step seemed part of the program. I found myself exiting the elevator running toward my unit not caring how much noise I made. I unlocked the front door and turned the knob abruptly. I had to reach the balcony before my parents could stir. Before they wake I would have already landed on the ground.

After I threw the balcony door open, I stretched out my arms and dangled most of my upper body over the railing. The scenery suddenly changed. I saw how far down the ground was. It would be a dive into a bottomless pit . . . I would die . . . an actualization of my worst nightmare. *I don't want to die; I am still scared of death.* Instantly, I was human again.

I walked back to the living room and heard my mom's voice trembling from their bedroom. "There . . . is . . . is . . . a thief . . . in . . . our home." Then, I saw my dad's head lurking behind the door. He had a quick peek toward my direction. He must have seen a monstrous shadow standing in the dark, a scene from a horror movie. He slammed the door and screamed, "Go away, we are calling 911!" His voice was so creepy, goose bumps poked out all across my skin. The very reason they were scared was because there was no telephone in their bedroom.

"Baba! Mama! It's me!" My desire for death totally vanished.

"Xia Xi!" My parents ran to me and held me so tight as if they would never let go of me. They must have figured out why I came home.

"Baba, Mama, I still could not get any sleep. I did not sleep at all. I feel extremely suicidal! I cannot help it!"

"No, no, no, you cannot do this to us. We cannot live without you!" We tangled up into a howling ball.

My dad phoned my friend's house. "Err . . . sorry to wake you up . . . Nancy walked home . . . Yes, she is home right now." I could feel the shockwave penetrating the receiver from the other end. My dad continued, "Sorry about this . . . The truth is, she has been feeling very down lately, she really needs someone to comfort her. Nancy said being with her good friend makes her happy. We thought she would feel better boarding at your home for a while . . . No, she did not get any sleep. It is more serious than we thought . . . I am so sorry . . . Okay, thank you so much!" After he hung up, he immediately called his brother in China, "Brother, Xia Xi wants to commit suicide! The fortune-teller was right! I don't know what to do now . . ." he wept bitterly.

I did not hear the rest of the conversation because my mom took me to my bed. She rocked me in her arms like I was a child again. I looked upward at her, her reddened eyes were begging for my compassion. She had not had a good night sleep since my insomnia started. I had been tormenting everyone, Mom and Dad and of course, myself. How could I stop this brutality? I began to feel drowsy. The warmth of her cradle brought me to a complete rest.

2

I slept for the first time in three weeks, but I woke up without feeling refreshed. My thoughts immediately picked up speed and brought back this unbearable headache. When I walked out of my room, my dad called me, "I am not going to work for now. I will accompany you every day and talk you out of your problem. This is a crisis and we will deal with it together." I saw a lot of confidence in his eyes. Did he really think this is a problem that he can "talk me out of"? The kind of evil force reigning over me was way out of his league.

After breakfast, my dad brought me to Bluffer's Park. We walked slowly along the beach. The balmy sun and the breezy air made a perfect couple. The gorgeous weather suddenly magnified my depression. My dad led me toward a bush of wild flowers. They were blossoming in their prime. "Look how beautiful they are! How beautiful life is. Isn't life worth living?" I replied silently, *yes, they are beautiful, but I don't think anything beautiful is made for me.*

We sat down on a bench facing the peaceful lake. A little boy was flying his kite. His dog was running after him. There was an old man sitting not far from the boy, calling after him to be careful. My dad said, "Look, we will have a life like that. We will be happy again. I know you always want a dog. I promise I will get you one." As I stared at the smile on that boy's face, I was jealous of his pure and genuine happiness, a reflection of a life without hurt, sorrow, and of course, depression. His dog was even more eye-catching. It was jumping up and down and furiously wagging its tail. That son of a bitch was better off than me.

"Dad, last night I heard you say something about the fortune-teller. What did you mean by that?" My dad sighed. "I never believed in things like that . . . The year when we were applying for immigration, I met a fortune-teller on the street. I was with my friends at the time. A man approached us and insisted on telling me my fortune. I said I was not interested. Meanwhile, my friends wanted to hear theirs. The fortune-teller ignored them and said he only wanted to do business with me. I was persuaded by his determination. He told me that the year 1998 would be a turning point for me, which was true because we were about to come to Canada. He also predicted that when I turn forty-five years old, something will happen to my child. He did not know what." He paused for a few seconds, "He also said whatever it is, she will get over it." I was stunned. *Is this whole thing meant to happen? Did he really say I would "get over it"?* My dad thought of something and chuckled. "Why are you laughing, Dad?" "The fortune-teller also predicted that I would be extraordinarily wealthy." He said it with sarcasm.

After we left the park, my dad drove me to a temple. It was a place of worship for many of his Chinese coworkers. Although I never knew much about the Christian God, I always believed there was something out there, some supernatural being that had a lot of power and authority over mankind. I was pretty sure that this big boss had no affection for me. As we stepped into the dimmed temple, I felt a chill penetrating my flesh. There was a spell in the air, mystic and spooky. I saw three wooden statues of idols towering at the center. They looked horrifying with their eyes wide open. They were holding some kind of object that reminded me of my elementary school teacher with her spanking ruler. An invisible force in the temple weakened my knees and compelled me to bow. I felt like if I were to stare at the idols for one more second, they would punish me and make my life even more miserable than it already was. I dropped to my knees on one of the mats and pressed my face against the floor. I could almost taste the dust and dirt. I sobbed quietly, "Please help me get over this, please help me, please help me . . ." Then, I bowed and bowed like the way I saw worshippers did on TV.

3

I continued to suffer from insomnia. The pace of my thoughts was firing like a machine gun, executing every cell in my brain. My head was aching beyond reason. I felt like a monster was furiously growing underneath my skull, pounding and cracking my lobes. Every insomniac night made that creature beefier and lousier.

My mom was sleeping by me every night. Every toss and turn of mine would awaken her. She was like a puppet and I was her master. The strings on her body were twitching along with my movement. Once every half hour, she would sit up and lightly pat my chest, "Don't think of anything, try to calm down, let your mind go blank." When dawn came, she slowly rose from her bed and dragged her weariness to work. I had no idea how she managed to go to work without any rest at night. "Don't worry about me. I will eat lunch quickly and sleep during the rest of the break. I am able to fall asleep." I heard her say that to my dad before going to work, "I will sleep beside her tonight." My dad offered to take her place. "No, you snore very loud. Plus, if you fall asleep, you cannot watch her, what if she . . ." The rest was said in a whisper.

During the day, my dad was glued onto me. He was guarding every move I made. All the knives in the kitchen were hidden from my reach. The handle of the balcony door was wired shut. Common sense told me that the quickest way would be to jump off a subway platform or throw myself over a highway bridge, but part of me was afraid of the pain and torture before dying. Death mocked me for being a coward. The act of living was not easy, but I didn't expect death would be this hard too. I started searching on the Internet for inspirations. Hopefully, people would share their "recommended" methods to commit suicide. I needed an easy way out of this world, instant and painless. But as it turned out, all the websites I went to were trying to talk people out of their suicidal ideation. I didn't want to read them anymore. I didn't want my determination to waver.

One day, while my dad was on the phone with his brother, I opened my mom's closet and rummaged through her drawers. There, buried under layers of clothes, I found a bottle of sleeping pills pre-scribed for my insomnia. It was newly obtained from the pharmacy. Sixty pills were inside the bottle. *Perfect.*

Before bedtime, I wrote a farewell note to my parents. I told them how sorry I was for forsaking them. I wished that they would carry on after my death and have another child to replace me. The words were a bunch of bullshit inspired by cheesy soaps. After fold-ing that piece of paper under my pillow, I was ready.

That night, I acted like I had finally "snapped out of my depres-sion". I told my parents all the wonderful lies and successfully con-vinced my mom to sleep in her own room. Right before bedtime, I locked myself in the bathroom, poured out all of the pills and shov-eled them down at once. I choked. I spat out a mouthful and swal-lowed them in three smaller lots. Suddenly I regretted everything, just like that night on the balcony. The last sliver of sanity was strug-gling to keep me alive. I then thrust my fingers down my throat to retrieve the pills. I vomited at least ten pills into the toilet. They were wrapped with thin strings of blood. *Should I call for help? It's still not too late to change my mind* . . . The last thing I remembered was walking back to my room, the moment I laid my body down, I was out of this world . . .

Next morning, I woke up! I tried to get up, but quickly realized my body had lost all of its strength. My fingers were as weak as strings of cooked noodles. I was dizzy and the world was spinning above me.

Ironically, after a night of deep sedation, my brain finally caught a break. My desire to die was replaced by my instinct to live. I wanted to live again. Then I called my dad and told him about consuming the pills last night. He slapped me across the face, but I was too numb to feel any pain. He scolded me in a trembling voice, "Look at you! Where is my daughter! You are *not* her!" He wanted to take me to the hospital right away. My legs were too weak to walk and I was too heavy to be carried. He wrapped my arm around his shoulder like a solider helping a comrade and dragged me all the way through the corridor, the elevator and into the garage. He was crying and cursing every step of the way. On the road to the hospital, I dozed off again on the backseat.

When we arrived at Scarborough Grace Hospital, we were turned back by two paramedics. I vaguely heard that the hospital was closed because it was infected with SARS, a serious pandemic which had originated in China. It was a lethal air-borne disease that had already killed several patients and health care professionals in and around Toronto. The city, the country and the world were as chaotic as my tiny universe.

The two paramedics decided to take me in their ambulance to another hospital located about twenty minutes away. As one drove, the other one began to measure my blood pressure and other vital signs. He seemed nice. Gently he asked me about what had happened. I shamelessly told him the truth, "My boyfriend broke up with me." This was the reason everyone in my life believed in. *But did I really die for love? If he were to take me back, would that be my remedy?* The paramedic comforted me by saying, "You are only eighteen. You will soon move on." *I will soon move on* . . . I wanted to believe him so badly.

When we arrived at Centenary Hospital, I was placed in a wheelchair and pushed to the triage nurse. Unlike the paramedic, this female nurse was devoid of compassion. She asked me the same question in a rigid voice, "Why did you do what you did?"

"My boyfriend broke up with me." I curled into a ball, not wanting to face her cold and judgmental look.

"How long were you together?"

"About one month."

"WHAT!"

I felt a big wave of shame drowning me.

"Did you think of killing another person?"

"Yes." For some reason I was more honest than I needed to be.

"Who?"

"Will."

"How did you think of killing him?"

". . . I don't know." This time I lied.

The sleeping pills I took were the mildest type. It did not do any lasting damage to my brain and body. In fact, the only treatment required was to wait for the drug to urinate out of my system. Later that day, I was admitted to the observation unit. At bedtime, I told my nurse, "I have insomnia. I need some sleeping pills to help me sleep." She laughed, "You still have a lot in you."

That first night in the hospital, I managed to get an extremely shallow sleep for at least three hours. A stream of laughter entered my consciousness from the nursing station. *Are they mocking me? Are they talking about how stupid I am?* I used to be a mean-spirited person. I used to despise people who resorted to suicide. I thought they were cowards, but now . . . *Karma is a damn bitch.* I began to recall all the ugly things I had done and said against other people. My mind was roused again. My resurrected ability to sleep died its second death.

The next morning, my mom came to visit me. The thick bags under her eyes were hard to ignore. She looked like she'd aged ten years. Though I knew I was the only person who could save her, I was powerless to save myself. "Because of SARS, Dad is not allowed to visit today. He will come tomorrow." She paused for second, "We cry every time when we see your empty bed. Xia Xi, we need you. We cannot live without you. You have to live for us. I am begging you. Can you assure me that you will not do anything to hurt yourself again?" I said nothing but simply nodded. I did not want to make any empty promises. She took out two books our relatives mailed to me from China, "See this woman? She was trying to end her life at one point. I have highlighted some of the words in this book which will definitely help you." Then, she started reading . . . All of those words had already been said by so many people too many times. *I know the value of life, I know how much my parents love me, I know I am only eighteen, I know the reason for my suicide is ridiculous.* I had heard all the inspirational quotes that mankind could offer. In fact, I could give a lecture to a whole bunch of depressed people on why they should not be depressed.

The sleeping pills were out of my system by the time night arrived and my insomnia had returned to its full potency. Death once again closed its grip on me . . .

The next day, I was moved to a psychiatric ward for juveniles. Before I entered the door, I saw a lunatic wandering in the adult ward. He was wearing nothing but a hospital gown. Half of his butt was dangling outside. *I'd rather die than becoming someone like him.*

I was given a single room with a large window that looked out to the street and the parking lot. The facility was cozy and tidy, definitely favorable as a break from the outside world. I could not tell if there was anything wrong with my fellow patients. They all appeared to be normal. Some of them even looked happy.

That afternoon, while I was playing with a jigsaw puzzle in the lounge, a young nurse came to me and sat beside me. At first, she was helping me with finding the puzzle pieces and we talked about trivial things. After warming up, she began her real mission. She tried to be assertive, but there was no other way to do it without pinching my most sensitive nerve, "How long were you together?"

"One month."

She must have read my file. It wasn't surprising to her. Very carefully she asked again, "Was it very intense? Did you . . ." I violently swung my head to stop her from completing the question. *No, technically we did not have sex.*

The nurse continued, "Do you know that depression is treatable? Sometimes, thoughts of suicide are temporary. A lot of people we've seen only attempted once and recovered eventually. It takes time and patience."

"How long will it take me to feel better?"

"You are on medications now. In at least two months or so you should feel the effects."

"Two months!" I was startled. It had only been a month since my depression, I already felt like I had been in this bloodbath for life.

"Yes, part of the work depends on the medication; the other part depends on you. You have the power to overcome this." Everyone kept on telling me I could overcome my depression with will power. Well, at least this nurse only expected me to meet her half way.

Later that day I saw my father. He looked even more broken than Mom. He took my hands and said, "We talked to your uncle in Washington DC, he said it would be beneficial to take you on a vacation. That's what a lot of people do when they are stressed. After you are discharged from this hospital, we will drive to his city. It has the most amazing museums in the world. You will be fascinated and you will forget about all your problems." That actually sounded like a great idea. Indeed, that is what a lot of people do after a dramatic breakup. They go away on a vacation, shop like there is no tomorrow, drink like the world is ending, defile their body to finish off their bucket list, and come back redeemed. It might just be the cure for me. I had a flicker of hope.

When Dad left, I sat beside the large window and looked at the world I almost left behind: the still parking lot, the busy traffic, the beautiful sunset . . . *Where would I be at this time if I had been successful?* Suddenly, I saw my dad exiting the hospital and walking toward a plaza where his car was parked. With all that happened he tried to save a little money and not pay for hospital parking. Tears welled up in my eyes looking at the way he tiredly placed one foot in front of the other. He looked so alone. "I am so sorry," I mumbled. It was as if he heard me . . . he stopped, turned around, looked up and waved. He put up a smile for me. It was impossible to see his face clearly but I was positive that hope was also in his eyes.

The next day I was discharged and met with the psychiatrist one last time. She was wearing a mask as part of the protocol during SARS. All I could see was a pair of expressionless eyes. I was advised to continuously take my medications. The doctor warned that going away would not make me better because this had to do with a chemical imbalance in my brain, a concept that was foreign to me. She did not offer any further explanation. I wanted more encouragement, such as "You will recover for sure" or "I guarantee you will be happy again." But I guess she too, did not want to give empty promises.

4

After coming back from the hospital, it was déjà vu all over again. I was still unable to sleep. My brain was like a pool of sewage, overflowing with thoughts of shame and regret. In order to channel my excessive amount of mental energy, I started to talk nonstop, mostly meaningless mumbo-jumbo. I also had difficulty with being still. I was constantly walking around and pacing in circles. I finally knew why lunatics needed to be tied up and caged. The antidepressants seemed ineffective, so I stopped taking them.

Without sleeping, my hormonal system began to rebel. My skin was oily and my hair was greasy. I noticed the facial hairs on my upper lip had grown noticeably thicker and darker. I used to bleach them religiously as part of my beauty regimen, but now I just let them take over. I remembered all the things I used to do to make myself pretty. I thought a pretty girl could get whatever and whoever she wanted. I now realized that all of my previous confidence was based on my look. As I peeked at my disfigured reflection in the mirror, I felt like a piece of trash, a lifeless soul clothed by an ugly cover. My human essence had already died. My flesh needed to follow. *I need to die.* It was a biological need, far surpassing the need for water, food, and sex. I would not care about dying as a virgin.

The following two weeks were exam period, my grade twelve final exams. With all the conditional offers I received from various universities, I needed to maintain my current average in order to be officially accepted, but I knew I did not have the mental capacity to do any studying. On top of that, I had missed too many classes in the past month.

"Dad, I don't want to go back to school. I cannot face those people. They probably know everything that has happened. They've been making fun of me ever since I got dumped. I am so embarrassed. I don't want to go to school." My dad sighed. "Do your best, I will try to talk to your principal again." The fact is, he had met with my principal several times since the night I walked home from my friend's house. He had been asking if it would be possible to submit current marks as my final marks. My dad was hoping that my chance of going to university would not be affected. The principal was firm that this was unprecedented, especially after finding out why I wanted to commit suicide. It seemed like all of the office staff despised us. We became notorious. The principal began to avoid my dad who was often left waiting in vain. My father believed in honest labor and had never before begged anyone for a favour. But this time he was willing to do anything for his only child, absolutely anything and everything. Bowing his head and swallowing his pride seemed a trivial sacrifice.

On the day of my Geometry exam, I arrived purposely late when everyone had already started. I sneaked in meekly and kept my head down. My teacher passed me the exam paper and gave me a look of encouragement. He was my favorite teacher. My mark before this point was in the 90s. As I read the exam questions, I was completely defeated. Each number and symbol looked like they were jumping off the paper and dancing the victory dance. Will walked in at that moment; he was purposely late as well. Seeing him gave me a mild heart attack. I wanted to leave. I wanted to leave the classroom before anyone else. My teacher spoke to me softly, "You must be able to do more than that. Just write something."

When the exam was over, my principal was waiting for me outside of the classroom. He led me out of the school to meet up with my dad. "We will submit your marks as what they are right now and you can be exempted from the rest of the exams, but we need a note from a psychiatrist."

"Thank you!" I said in tears.

"Good luck to you." The principal rigidly shook our hands and quickly walked back to the building.

I felt a huge relief. I never have to go to school again; never have to see people I don't like and never ever have to see Will again. *Out of sight, out of mind.* In the absence of my stressors, I would probably start recovering. For a split second, I felt . . . happy—something I almost forgot how it felt.

My best friend Teresa took me to her church twice. The first time was on a Christmas Eve. I was there for the free turkey dinner. At the end, the pastor asked us if anybody in the congregation would like to open their heart to Jesus. Teresa nudged me and gave me a wink. Under her peer pressure, I stood up against my own will. As part of the deal, I went to church on the following Sunday. I felt even more forced this time. I paid no attention during the sermon. In reaction to hearing things that were cheesy and absurd, I would roll my eyes or stick out my tongue. I never wanted to go to church again. Yet the strangest thing was, every single time I thought about suicide, the thought of going to church immediately countered it. These two ideas were at constant battle in my head. Was God the antagonist of my demise? I wanted to try Him. I asked my dad to take me to Teresa's church after leaving school. If a pastor were to lay his hands on me and pray for me, perhaps I could be miraculously cured. But that afternoon, we were told that the pastor was absent due to a family emergency. *Had God denied me because I had denied Him first?* Then I walked into the empty chapel, gazing up at the cross hanging at the center of the altar. It was then I realized that I had no idea what it meant. I used to see it as nothing but a pendant, nothing but a fashion accessory. Never before did I have the interest to find out its real significance. Somehow at that moment, I was desperate to know it better, the whole deal of Jesus, God, and the Cross. How could that rugged Cross possibly save a wretch like me?

5

Time had come for us to head to Washington DC in the name of healing. At that point, it had become a ridiculous idea. Nothing in this world could bribe me to stay, not even an acceptance letter from the most prestigious university, not even a love letter from the most gorgeous prince. While my parents were packing and talking about sightseeing in DC, I had a different plan in mind. Perhaps the capital city of the most powerful nation would be my final destination. I would surely cause a scene and be remembered as someone who had once lived.

In the last two months, I had tried my best to sleep every night. But the night before our trip, I intentionally stayed awake. I kept my eyes staring blankly into the darkness and brainstorming different ways to die. During that productive eight hours, I had come up with several scenarios. The most creative one was hijacking my dad's steering wheel on the highway leading to our common grave.

When I rose in the morning, I was greeted by my parents' hope and excitement, "We just called your uncle and aunt. They have already made plans for us. They are so happy to see us. With their help, you will feel better for sure!" I asked myself, *wouldn't it be easier if I jump off the balcony right now?* I quietly walked toward the balcony and discovered that the door handle was wrapped by wires. There was no way I could break it free without tools. "Let's go! I hope to arrive before dinner time." My dad broke my thought and hurried me out of the door.

While he was concentrating on driving, I slowly unbuckled my seat belt. I had no intention to jump out of the car, but I was hoping that if we were in a car collision, I would be killed with dignity. Before taking actions of my own volition, maybe I could create the illusion of an "accidental" death.

They say in the moments before death you see flashbacks of your life, all the great and small events playing like a slideshow. But in my case, it was a voluntary process. On our road to Washington DC, I purposely engaged myself in recollection . . .

I was born with a sinful nature. As a baby, I was extremely demanding and restless. It was hard to take care of me or simply put me to sleep. As a child, I was a pessimistic introvert, crying over the pettiest adversary and seeing the worst in every situation. I had this phobia and ill obsession about death. I had wasted a great amount of time thinking about the apocalypse or the annihilation of the human race. I was way too complicated as a kid.

In elementary school, I was a brilliant student. My marks were always in the top five. However, during my last exam, I got 290 out of 300, which were 3 marks short of making it into an "Ivy League" junior high school. After attending a local school for a semester, I was completely changed. My marks dropped significantly as I began my downward spiral to rebellion. I made several attempts to challenge the authorities and rules in my life. I even got caught cheating on a test. That was one of the major reasons my parents decided to immigrate to Canada. They were already in their forties at the time. It'd be difficult to start from scratch in a foreign country where we knew absolutely nobody, but they were determined.

Our first year in Canada was filled with stress and obstacles. Language was the biggest barrier. My parents could not find jobs that were compatible with what they used to do in China. In order to make living, they became general laborers each working in a factory. They left for work when it was still dark outside, and when they returned home, the sun had set. For the first few years, we could not afford a decent apartment. We had to live in other people's basement. The lack of sun exposure made my mom's health decline.

I constantly experienced prejudice as a newcomer from mainland China. The sad part was, it wasn't people of other races and colors that hurt me the most; it was people who came from Taiwan and Hong Kong. They identified themselves as "Taiwanese" or "Hong-Kongnese" but not "Chinese." Being extremely sensitive was not helping; it'd take me forever to get over the hurt of an insult. Often times, I'd lose sleep at night.

As I grew older, I envied other girls in school who had found boyfriends. I was jealous of seeing couples holding hands, making out, and shamelessly parading their romance in public. While in grade eleven, I was in the same class with a Korean boy. I liked him the first time I saw him. He'd make my day by a single glance or smile. Gradually, I felt like the feeling was mutual. We went on a date to the movies and watched Mr. Deeds. On our way home, our moving bus suddenly came to a stop. I lost balance and almost fell. The way I swung my leg in the air made everyone on the bus laughing hysterically. I saw him giggled too. I had never been more embarrassed. Afterward, I had no courage to talk to him again. That was the end of our short-lived relationship. We never kissed, never held hands, and never shared a hint of impurity, but he was my first love.

In grade twelve, Will entered into my life. He was in five of my six classes. He was tall and cute. It was an instant attraction. I made it obvious that I was pursuing him. It changed me into someone who liked to flaunt her sex appeal. I began to wear tight clothes and spent most of my savings on shoes, clothes and makeup. I focused all my energy and resources on appearance. As time went by, I became obsessed and delirious over him. Although I managed to do all my homework and maintain a good mark, the rest of my time was wasted on how to make my next move on Will. Finally, I asked him out over the phone. He said, "Okay."

I was perfectly aware of how this relationship began to influence me mentally. I was not able to concentrate in class. I had no interest in doing homework. I got an unprecedented seventy on a geometry test. I did not care. I was thinking about Will all the time, reliving our past moments, savoring our present and fantasizing about the future. The pace of my thinking started to quicken. My sleep became shallow. Sometimes, I got no sleep at all.

Four weeks later, I got dumped. Everyone in school saw it coming before we even started dating. It hit me hard. I fell from the highest high to the lowest low. I did what I could to get over Will including making out with a boy at a party. His mouth was filled with remnants of Doritos chips. His grip on my breasts was cruel. When he wanted to go further, I told him "I am on my period right now.""Ewwwww!" That was the end of it. Before long, my slutty reputation began to spread among the insiders. People's previous contempt was justified. Everything went wrong to generate the perfect storm. Insomnia began to chew on my brain. As the nights turned to day and the week passed I began feeling suicidal.

My poor parents, I feel so guilty, we had finally settled down in Canada, but just when they thought they had begun a smooth sail, I dragged them into a new voyage in the ocean of fire . . .

7

About half way on the road to Washington, I finished reminiscing. It wasn't much. After all, I had only lived eighteen years. Eighteen years. What if time could go back to 1985? Then I could be reborn, or perhaps never be born at all . . . Life's could-haves, would-haves and should-haves unchained another wave of suicidal impulses. A voice tempted me, "Grab that steering wheel. Do it!" It sounded just like my own, with the same pitch and accent. We were driving on a highway where there were barriers between opposing lanes. It was not how I had originally imagined it. I was selfishly hoping for a head-on collision with another car that would assure fatality. But now, *what if I survive the crash with a serious injury? What if my parents are killed instead of me?* Then a huge truck was driving beside us. As I stared at the size of those monstrous wheels, I suddenly realized that if I were to jump now those tires would mush me and spit my body all over the pavement. Then one after another the other vehicles would join in to tear my remains into millions of pieces. Death would be a guarantee, but . . . I was scared. I was *still* scared. There had to be a better way to die, there had to be . . .

By early evening, we arrived in DC. My uncle and aunt had been in the United States for over twenty years. Their house was located in a new neighborhood, where most of the nearby houses were still under construction. When I stepped out of the car the noises of construction assaulted me from all directions. The hammering and drilling aggravated my headache to a brand new level. It was also the hottest and most humid time in Washington. I felt like I just rolled into a cremator. This was the last place on earth for rehabilitation.

When my uncle and aunt met me at the door, they were stunned. Not having any sleep for over two months showed and it was obvious that something was very wrong with me. They did not expect to see me looking this bad. They hugged me. As I tried to smile back, I realized that depression had paralyzed the muscles on my face. My dad took my uncle aside to explain "the situation" in more detail. My uncle frowned.

After dinner, my aunt took me to her bedroom upstairs. She opened up to me about the most painful experience in her life. "During that dark period, I ran red lights several times. I would have been killed if there were other cars crossing the intersection. I truly understand how it feels to be heart-broken. But, everyone gets over it eventually." *Here we go again; everyone believes I want to die because of my broken heart.* I was certain that it was not about Will anymore. It was something else, something much more powerful and evil.

When it was my uncle's turn, he gave me a lecture on the value of life. "In history, thousands of people sacrificed themselves for the freedom and well-being of others. They died in a courageous way and were remembered forever. Everyone eventually dies, some people's death weighs heavier than mountains, some people's death is as light as feather. We cannot be the latter one, *blah . . . blah . . . blah . . .*"

My insomnia continued that night. I felt like my head was getting heavier and heavier. This headache was as explosive as a pissed-off volcano. I could feel the lava boiling and searing the last remnant of sanity. I had so much mental energy that I could not lay still. I had to get up and move around to feel less crazy. My dad came kneeling down in front of me and begging, "Please get some sleep, please get some sleep." As I looked at my parents under the dim moonlight—my insomnia had poisoned them with the same venom. They were a few sleepless nights away from a complete meltdown.

The next morning, my parents asked my uncle for directions to the most famous museums in the city. They still believed that having a fun trip would help me. This was pre-GPS era. It was not easy driving in a new city. I used to be my dad's navigator when we were travelling on the road. I'd sit beside him with a map and direct him to turn left or right. But this time, finding things on the map was like finding Waldo. I was helplessly feeble. "I want my daughter back . . . I want my daughter back . . ." My dad mumbled as tears came down from his eyes.

After a while, we finally arrived at the heart of the capital. Everywhere I looked was majestic and lofty. I felt like my presence just polluted this place. I dropped my head and stared at the ground as I was walking. Other pedestrians explicitly wanted to flee away from me. People in nearby cars kept on honking at us, as though we were lepers, and they wanted to chase us off their holy land. We saw a beggar sitting on the street. My dad gave me a coin and signaled me to give it to the beggar. This had become a new practice. Somehow he believed that being generous would bring healing to me. As I threw the coin in the beggar's cup, he immediately looked the other way in disgust. He was the superior one between us. Indeed, he was. He was begging to stay alive, whereas I would give up everything in exchange for death.

When we stepped into the Smithsonian National Air and Space Museum, we immediately became the focus of people's attention. They were frightened. Crowds began to spread around us. We were like Moses parting this sea of people. A little white girl saw me walking toward her. She appeared to be extremely agitated. Her phobic expression reminded me of a childhood trauma when I saw rats running around in our kitchen. I had made the exact same face then. I suddenly felt an itch in my throat, I coughed. A lady cursed and immediately dragged her boyfriend as far away as she could. That's when I remembered the SARS pandemic. It started around the same time of my depression, but I had lost track of its progress. Being a

Chinese and looking this sick, it was reasonable to assume that I had SARS. How I wished I could be a real SARS patient, die a death that had at least some kind of meaning.

After we came out of the Museum, we entered a mall to look for a bathroom. At first, my dad wanted to ask a middle-aged man. As soon as the man saw my father approaching, he turned around and walked away. My dad went to a security guard. "I don't know!" was her reply. At last, he asked a janitor. The janitor vaguely pointed toward the direction of the bathroom before returning to his chore— we were rejected by the whole world. My outing concluded with an even stronger determination to commit suicide.

At dinner time, my uncle was quiet at the table. My aunt was trying to act natural as if I was still the niece she once knew. After dinner, she gave me a brand-new Bible. She had been a Christian for years. "During my toughest time, when I found it hard to sleep, I would read Psalms. You will find comfort in God's Words." Then, she put her hand on me and prayed for me. She was asking God to restore me. It was the first time I attentively listened to someone's prayer. It sounded like she was asking God to grant wishes as if He was a "genie in the bottle." *No wonder religious people are gullible and foolish.*

That evening, my aunt wanted to take me to a fellowship meeting. She had only met the hostess once or twice before. As we were driving, my aunt appeared to be nervous as she was constantly wiping her damped palms on her pants. It took her a while to find out that her handbrake was still on. At first, she could not find the correct street. She pulled into a gas station for directions. "Stay in the car, okay! Don't go anywhere." She walked away in apprehension. Before she entered the hut, she turned back to see if I was still in the car.

Finally, we found the house. When we stepped into it, people were surprised. They had not expected to see me. Nonetheless, they welcomed me whole-heartedly. We started the meeting by singing hymns in Chinese. Looking at the joyful expression in everyone else's face, I wondered what kind of God they were praising. I had never been to gatherings like this. If this scenario had happened prior to my depression, I would have despised it and considered it lame.

After singing, they began to read the Bible and discuss its meaning. I failed to register anything they said. My mind was absent; my spirit was homeless. However, the only thing I remembered was when a woman said, "On that final Judgment Day, God will sit on a white throne . . ."

That night, an inexplicable event took place. My insomniac volcano exploded. Literally, I felt like my brain blasted and shattered into million pieces. Blood that were previously accumulated in my head immediately streamed back to my body. My skull lost its content. I was now empty-headed, perfectly ideal to house every kind of demon. I departed even further from sanity. I curled into a corner and begged to my mom, "Kill me, I am begging you, if you love me, kill me please, I am begging you!" My mom's moist eyes were the only light in that pitch darkness.

The next day was my dad's 46th birthday. My aunt took me to the grocery store to prepare for his birthday celebration. At the entrance, we saw a stand displaying greeting cards. "Pick one and write a nice note to him." I randomly selected a card with *Happy Birthday* on it. Staring at the word *happy* was like being slapped across the face. While they were preparing for dinner, I was thinking about what to write on that card. "Happy Birthday, It's your 46th birthday, the fortune-teller said everything would pass and become better after this point. Your Daughter." A beautiful lie was the only birthday present I could get him. The dinner was eaten in an awkward silence. My parents were making fake smiles to appear like this was a lovey-dovey celebration. When I looked at them in that well-lit dining room, the wrinkles around their eyes were like spider webs. Their skin was dry and yellowish. The corners of their lips were saggy and hungered for a real smile. I saw two withered human beings slowly being roasted in this hell that I had lit for them.

After dinner, my parents told my uncle, "We will leave tomorrow. Apparently, she has not become any better. After we get back to Toronto, we will hospitalize her." My uncle nodded. After a long pause, he said sympathetically, "The two thousand dollars you borrowed from me years ago, you don't need to return it. We just bought a house, we don't have much. Here is five hundred dollars."

Rain came down like Niagara Falls on that night. In fact, it had been pouring every single night since we got here. I could not help but wonder, "Is heaven crying for me?"

8

The drive back to Toronto felt much shorter than it actually was. The moment I stepped into our unit, I flew to the balcony door. The handle was still tightly wired. I realized if I didn't get rid of my parents first, I would never be able to get outside. I quickly walked to the storage room and saw a hammer in the toolbox. I held it behind my back as I quietly approached my dad. When I was close enough to him, I raised the hammer and attempted to hit him at the back of his head. *I will surely be punished for this.* My dad heard something and quickly turned around. His eyes bulged out of the sockets as he saw the hammer coming down on him. It was effortless for him to catch my wrist in the air and snatch the hammer from my hand. My parents went hysterical. They held my hands tightly as if putting hand-cuffs on them. They cried as they dropped their knees in front of me, "Are you trying to kill us too! We are as good as dead if you are not in this world! How could this be! Where is our daughter? Wake up! Please wake up!" I was indifferent to their pleas. I looked out the window with my lifeless stare, formulating plan B, C, and D. "Do you even cry now?" My dad was stunned by my lack of emotion. *Good question.* I realized I stopped crying long time ago. I was incapable to love or sympathize, and I was no longer even sad or depressed. Indeed, I was devoid of any primitive emotions. I was inhuman and even less than an animal. My existence was a waste of oxygen.

Believe it or not, I slept that night. It felt like a coma that wiped away eight hours of my life. When I opened my eyes again, it was already the morning of June 20, 2003. My mom greeted me with a smile I had not seen for a long time. "Xia Xi, you were snoring last night! It is a sign that you are getting better. Oh I am so thankful! Eventually this will pass. We made an appointment to see the family doctor. He will tell us which hospital we should go to. We think it's best for you to stay in the hospital for a while. Get ready! We have the first appointment today." *There's absolutely no way I am going to a hospital. They will lock me in an asylum. Like how it is in movies, they will chain me up and treat me like an invalid. Oh yes, I am an invalid, I will never be normal again. I have to die, I must die!*

I walked out of my room, still in my pajamas and headed to the balcony door. I yanked the handle violently, trying to force it to open. My dad immediately approached. I came up with a scheme. In a very calm voice, I said, "Dad, I want to get some fresh air. It is a beautiful morning. I will be hospitalized for a while; I want to get some fresh air before that." That was the most rational statement I had made in months. He paused for a few seconds and said, "Okay, I trust you." Even I was surprised that he could be tricked this easily. (Later in life, he recalled that his mind was a blur at that moment. He had no idea why he believed me.) My dad walked back to the storage room and took out a pair of pliers. He began to cut the wires loose. A few seconds later, the door was open. The first thing I saw was a chair. I used to sit on it to watch the sunrise. Who knew it would one day become my chariot to the underworld. I forcefully tried to brush off my dad's hand, and as soon as I was able to unchain from him, I stepped onto that chair and hopped over the railing without a single second of hesitation. My dad could not have come any faster. He slammed his chest onto the railing—*BANG!* A sound that was louder than thunder. He caught a small part of my pants and suspended me in midair for a second . . .

More than a dozen times, my dad described to me how it was like on the day I was born. The nurse brought me out of the delivery room. She spread my legs open, without being congratulatory, she said, "It's a daughter, okay?" "A daughter is better." My dad carefully held me in his arms and suddenly felt the indescribable joy of being a father. I opened my eyes for the first time and looked upward to meet his. On the day of my birth, the first person I saw was my dad, and ironically, he became the last person I saw on what I believed to be my doomsday.

Three seconds later, I landed on a bed of soil. It was soft and puffy, ready to plant flowers, ready to nurture new lives. I remained completely conscious. The second my back impacted the ground, all sensations from the waist down abandoned me. That was the day I learned about the absolute power of the spinal nerves. Even without any previous knowledge, I knew I would never be able to walk again. I saw a man standing beside me, looking down on me. He must have witnessed the whole thing. However, he was remarkably calm, as though he had been waiting for me to descend from the sky. He dialed 9-1-1.

Soon, I saw my parents were stumbling toward me screaming and wailing. My mom was holding our home phone in her hand. The frantic expression on her face made me realize that I owed her so much that I would never be able to pay her back. My dad didn't have the strength to hold up his body. He was crawling on the ground like a slow stream of mud. Seeing them going officially crazy, I just found another reason to die.

When the paramedics arrived, one of them rubbed her hands against my thighs, "Can you feel this?" She asked in a professional tone. I felt a tingling sensation, but that was it. They placed me onto a stretcher and put an oxygen mask on me. On my way to Sunnybrook hospital, I did not feel like I was anywhere near death. They did not even sound the sirens! Disbelief and anger overwhelmed me. *How could I have survived? Eighth floor was not high enough? JEEZE! I should have run in front of a car! I should have jumped off the subway! I should have never left my mother's womb! Oh how I curse the day I was born!*

The rest of the day went by in a blur. I could not remember what was real and what was delusion. But somehow, I fell into a deep, deep sleep on that night.

9

I woke up. *Where am I? Who am I?* My mind was empty as a newborn's. It took a while to remember everything and the horror attached. There was a thin tube in my nostrils, supplying oxygen to me. I tried to pull it out, but my hands were tied up to the bed rails. I looked around and saw myself in a regular hospital room. I had a roommate, an elderly woman.

A psychiatrist came. She untied me and said, "We did a scan on your brain, there was nothing wrong with it." She then passed me a sheet of paper and asked me to copy three images: a circle, a rectangle and a more complex geometric drawing. I completed them perfectly. She then asked me to write a sentence, any sentence. I wrote in Chinese, "Baba, Mama, I am sorry." She went out of the room. I heard someone translate the message into English. She returned and said, "You will start taking antidepressants and we will place you on suicide watch."

My parents came to see me. They were the last two people on earth that I wanted to see. I could not imagine how they had spent the night. Their eyes were all swollen. They were so exhausted that they could barely talk. My dad lifted up his shirt and showed me the bruises on his chest; they were colorful like a painter's palette. It was the result of him banging against the balcony railing. He also showed me a broken knuckle, bent at a bizarre angle. It was injured three seconds before I injured my spinal column. It would serve as a constant reminder of my ultimate betrayal.

I had two attendants per day, each having a twelve-hour shift, watching my every move 24/7. They also performed some basic cares such as feeding, giving me a sponge bath and emptying my urine bag. One morning, my attendant was a middle-aged black woman. She had an aura of warmth and kindness. She introduced herself and wanted to know something about me. Her friendliness prompted my honesty.

"I jumped off a building, trying to kill myself."

"Oh Dear Lord!"

"That's right; your Lord is punishing me."

"Oh no, dear, God never punishes people. Oh dear!"

She then closed her eyes, raised her hand high up in the air and uttered her prayers in a theatrical style. She was a nerdy Christian reminding me of Ned Flanders from *the Simpsons*. "Oh Lord, please have mercy on this child . . ." Her prayer failed to resonate with me, not a word, but it was actually the first time I saw someone praying with such intensity and passion. She rubbed my hand back and forth to give me comfort. I was in desperate need of this shallow touch of understanding.

When I fell, one of my ribs slightly poked my lung, which caused some internal bleeding. A chest tube was inserted to drain blood from my wounded chamber. On July 1, 2003, thirteen days after the injury, it was time to pull the tube out before undergoing a major surgery to place rods and screws along my broken spinal column. However, it was not a smooth sail. When the doctor pulled the tube from my lung, I inhaled at that exact second. Immediately, I found it impossible to breathe. The pace of my breathing became rapid. I was panting like a dog, but I still felt like no oxygen had entered me. In order to restore the vacuum in my lung, the doctor located a practicable gap between my two ribs and punched another tube into my lung. I witnessed the entire process in awe. The restoration was not immediate. Even by the time visiting hours were nearly over, it was still a torture to breathe. My parents were crying bitterly. They worried that my surgery might be postponed as a result. "Xia Xi! If it's possible, we will suffer in your place. We are willing to do anything for you; we are willing to die for you!" As they were comforting me, I made a big effort to put another dagger into their heart. I used all of my energy to scream, "Please kill me!" Once again, they left the hospital in despair. I felt a strange sense of enjoyment in seeing them suffer. It was their fault for giving birth to a monster.

I was sleepless throughout the night. Every tormenting breath was forcing me to stay alive, and forcing me to live in failure and shame. Eventually, my breathing calmed and returned to normal by dawn. The surgery would proceed as scheduled. My parents were rejoicing when they saw me in the morning. My dad said, "Last night, my coworker and two other people from his church came to our home. They were praying for today's surgery. They stayed till almost 11p.m. Those are good people." His eyes watered. I had never seen a man cry this easily. Then, he posted Psalm 23 on the wall. "The Lord is my Shepherd, I shall not in want . . ." He read it out loud and explained to me the meaning of each verse. I remember how arrogant my dad used to be when people preached to him. He once pointed to the sky and taught me there was absolutely no God. But now, it seemed like he was willing to try anything and everything that might have some claim to save me. He wanted to rely on a God whom he had previously rejected with such conviction? *How ironic.*

The surgery lasted about six hours. It was a success. The actual damage to my spine was less severe than what it had appeared to be in the initial X-ray. The first memory I had when I woke up was finding myself in a dark room. As I was suffering from the aftereffects of anesthesia, I felt like my lower body was extremely heavy. The weight of the planet was tethered on me and dangling with Newton's gravity. The next form of torture was thirst. My mouth was unbelievably dry. It seemed like I was lost in a desert for millions of years. There was nothing else in my mind besides the sweet taste of rain and the soothing flow of water. "Water . . . Water . . . Please give me some water! I am begging you!" A nurse popped in, "You lost blood during the surgery, that's why you are thirsty. However, I cannot give you too much water because your internal organs are still numb. If you choke, you will not be able to cough it out." She was a nice nurse. She came back seconds later and used a wet cotton ball to moisturize my lips. She also gave me a cup of ice cubes, "Slowly melt this in your mouth. It should give some relief." I started chewing the ice cubes and rushed them down my throat. "Please give me more ice!" But I was denied this time. I began to fantasize the salvation of an oasis. I began to relive the memories of drinking a glass of ice-cold soda on a hot summer day. What surprised me was, at that moment, death was not my biggest longing.

10

False hope always takes advantage of hopeless people. One day, my dad brought a South-Asian woman to my room. She looked ordinary to me. My first guess was she must belong to a religious group that gives spiritual care to patients in the hospital. Unexpectedly, my dad called her "doctor". He said he bumped into a former patient in the lobby who introduced him to this woman. His paralysis was healed by her after "a few treatments". My dad immediately invited her upstairs to examine me. After touching my legs, feet and toes, she was very confident that she would be able to treat me. "You see, when I touch her foot like this, her toes curl up along with my hand movement." *Even a corpse could do that.* "Oh! Oh yeah! The toes are moving!" My parents were incredibly excited. "I will start my treatment when she is out of acute care." My dad accompanied her out of the room like a servant escorting a queen.

Ada was one of my attendants. She was about fifty years old. She stole my hospital food all the time. She'd take my tea bag and make tea for herself. She went through my tray to make sure nothing was wasted. Every other day or so, she'd ask the nurse to get me extra food and drinks, but at the end of her shift, she'd take them home. She was a scavenger feeding ghoulishly on the dying. Since Ada came most frequently, it was hard not to develop some kind of "bond" with her.

Occasionally, she would join the mockers' force, taunting and laughing at me for committing such stupidity, but during times when there was no other person in the room, I felt like she pitied me genuinely. When I asked her to rub my hand, she would caress it with motherly tenderness. One day, Ada called her teenage daughter and got into an argument. It was obvious that her rebellious daughter had no respect for her. She hung up the phone and sighed, "My daughter is in grade nine and she wants to move out with her boyfriend." Maybe she had no one to share her problems with or maybe because my family was also a pathetic mess, but that night, Ada began to disclose her heartaches to me. "My husband died five years ago in a car collision . . ." I instantly forgave her for everything.

Lee was one of my other attendants. She was a newcomer from China, having arrived in Canada less than a year ago. It was easy to start a chat with her in Mandarin. Like most immigrants, language was the biggest barrier for Lee and her husband. Since they could not do what they used to do in China, Lee's husband was too proud to look for low-paid blue-collar jobs. He stayed at home all day, doing nothing but being a pig. On the other hand, Lee was working two jobs. Besides being a Personal Support Worker, she also worked at a food court. Sometimes, after a night shift at the hospital, she had to attend her shift at the food court right away. There was no time to sleep. After comparing notes with me, she believed she also had symptoms of depression. "My biggest problem is loneliness. I don't have a friend in my life." Listening to her story, I thought about my dad. He was so willing to give up his pride to work as a general laborer. He used to make tofu in a cold factory. He used to unload cargo trucks in a warehouse. He was once injured after falling from the top of a stacking shelf. He went back to work without a full recovery because he thought he would lose his job. My poor dad . . . He used to say that he thought about me every time he had to lift a fifty-pound box to make a living. I was his only source of strength, but look at what I had done to him. I failed him miserably. Regret, guilt, pity, love, all of a sudden, I was overwhelmed with a mixture of emotions. *Emotions*, it had been ages since I had last felt something, anything.

11

Nerve pain started to wage war on me. I was under attack from all directions. I felt like a billion ants were nested inside my bones, chewing through my marrow. Every time this killer ache reached its maximum intensity, my eyeballs popped out of their sockets, my fingers twisted beyond logic. I hated the fact that it came and went without warning. I developed a psychological fear from anticipating its inevitable return. No break given, it was night and day, forcing me to stay in that agony of insomnia. I thought about the woe of labor. The excruciation was comparable, except I would not receive the joy of a new born as reward. I only gave birth to wind. I thought about God, a newly acquired concept; I thought about Him very, very often.

Trapped in bed all day every day, I set my mind free. I thought about the people I had hurt and the wrongs I had done. Thinking back, I was such a bad person—too many sins, countless lies and multiple cheats. I remembered this poor girl in my elementary school that came from a single-mother family. I bullied her for a few years. I called her "virus" and acted like if I was scared of being close to her. It was the exact reaction I received not long ago from people on the streets of Washington who thought I was a SARS patient.

Another distant memory also returned to shame me. This happened right before I came to Canada. One evening, I was hanging out with my friend after dinner. We saw a man and his young son walking toward us. The little boy was no more than four years old. After they passed us, they immediately turned around and caught up, "Excuse me, may I bother you for a second? We came from a village. My wife left us five years ago and came to Fuzhou to look for a job. She has not written to us for almost a year. I am trying to find her. This is the address to her place. This city is so big. I have no idea how to locate this address. Can you take a look?" My first thought was his wife probably dumped them. I had heard that happened all the time. Without even scanning the paper, I said, "We don't know it either, I am just a kid." "Perhaps, your parents can help us?" He was pleading. "We live far from here." In fact, I was only five-minutes walking distance from home. "Do you have fifty cents? My son has not eaten anything today. I want to buy him a bag of instant noodle." His son looked at me like a puppy nudging for a treat. I thought this was a beggar's scheme. I had my wallet with me, but instead, I said, "We did not bring any money. We are doing our leisure walk after dinner." Even though this contradicted to my previous statement about being far from home, I could not careless about hurting a villager's feeling. The man turned around abruptly and walked away in anger. That was his only means to save some dignity. My friend asked me quietly, "You have money, right?" "Yeah!" I didn't feel bad at all. At that time, I had no idea one day I would come to a rich country, where people treated me as if I came from a village.

After going through all my trespasses, I started to count the sins of my parents. They must have done something wrong to deserve this punishment. Yes, I remembered there was once, a child with an amputated arm came to us and begged for money. My mom attempted to walk away from him. The boy turned back to look at his mother. The woman signaled him to pursue us. When the boy touched my mom's coat, she shouted at him with fierce anger. The boy immediately began to cry. My mom quickly took off with me. Yes, that must be it. That was why her daughter became disabled.

God had taken vengeance for all those needy and poor people. Every sinister act was recorded. Not a single iniquity was overlooked.

Minutes later, my mom walked into my room. She just came from work. She was wet. It was raining outside. Out of the blue, I yelled at her with malice, "You are not a good person. You are evil!" She was stunned.

"Xia Xi, what's wrong?"

"You are evil! Dad is a bad person, too. You are bad people. That is why I became this way. I was punished. Do not come to visit me anymore. Do not come!"

"Xia Xi, tell Mom what happened?" She was sobbing without tears. She had no more tears after her prolonged grief.

My nurse came near and started to comfort my mom. This nurse was a sassy black lady. Two teardrops ran down her cheeks, but her voice was sharp like razor, "I feel for your mom. I feel for her! How can you say this to your own mother? What kind of person are you? You are unbelievable!"

My mom quickly recovered and began to do her routine tasks. She gathered some warm water in a basin and washed my face and hands with a soft towel. She took out the Chinese food she cooked in the morning and heated them in the kitchen. She fed me homemade food and ate my crappy hospital food. After eating, she took out a newspaper and read me articles of the day. Followed by a book borrowed from the library, in which she read me stories that are inspirational. After all that, she leaned on my bedside and soon fell into a nap. When she was asleep, her eyebrows were twisted into a frown. Her relaxed expression was a sad face by default.

During the SARS crisis, one of the hospital protocols was allowing only one visitor per day. Everyone had to wear a wristband in order to enter the hospital. My dad came to visit me every day after work. He'd sit in the car for my mom to come down, cut her wrist band off and tape it around his wrist. That way, he could sneak in and have a few minutes time visiting with me. That same evening my dad came up. He said with weariness, "Xia Xi, how could you say to your mother that she is a bad person? Why are you hurting her like that? Your mom gets up every morning before six, prepares food for the whole day. By the end of the day when we get home from the hospital, we usually don't have energy to cook. We just heat up whatever we have in the fridge. When we eat, we have to encourage each other to swallow the food. We have to keep ourselves healthy in order to take care of you . . . Your mom goes to work at seven in the morning, gets off at 11:00 a.m. and takes the bus for ninety minutes to come to see you. She is physically and mentally exhausted! Can't you tell by just looking at her? Do you know how much she loves you? She is willing to die for you! As for me, I don't even know why I go to work every day. I feel like my life has no purpose anymore . . . I feel like something is jammed up in my chest. I find it hard to breathe sometimes. It's a physical feeling. They say I should also seek counseling. I don't have time for that. I know they won't be helpful. You are the only one who can help me . . . I am not as strong as I thought I was. I just realized that. Your mom is even stronger than me. Xia Xi, please have pity on your parents. We came to Canada for you! We gave up our jobs in China so you could have a better future. You are our strength and motivation in everything we do. We cannot live without you. Please have some pity for your parents." His words cracked my stony heart. I started to cry. The warmth of my tears was a novel sensation on my face, "I am sorry, Dad, I . . . am so . . . sorry."

That was the first turning point.

12

One night, a fresh face came in. My attendant was a young African girl. Her smile was infectious. "My name is Irene! What's yours?" "Nancy." I replied. Unintentionally I returned her smile. I had not had a shower for more than a month. My hair smells like a breeding ground for some kind of organism. Even though she was not supposed to, Irene placed a bunch of towels under my head and shampooed my hair in bed. She gently massaged my skull, it felt so good. It had been too long since I last experienced any types of physical pleasure. I was deeply touched.

Irene had the night shift. After chatting for a while, it was bedtime for me. She grabbed my hand and said softly, "Do you know that I have come a long way from home? All of my families are in Africa. I pray every day for God's protection upon me and my loved ones. Let's have a bedtime prayer." She closed her eyes and I closed mine to imitate her. "Father . . ." I did not tune in to the rest of the prayer, but the instant I heard Irene call God "Father" I felt a quaking in my heart. Prior to that, I thought God was a sovereign judge with a rod and a whip in His hands. His wrath was impossible to satisfy. *But . . .God as a Father? To whom? Someone like Irene, who is merciful and kind to an undeserving person like me?*

Irene came again the next day, and the day after. She was my favorite attendant. Unlike most other attendants who would only watch me from a few meters away, Irene would sit beside my bed and chat with me like a friend.

Two months since the injury and two months after being placed on antidepressant, my sleep was restored. I was able to get at least four hours of quality sleep each night. Each yawning felt so familiar and so foreign. Gradually, death was no longer a necessity. If I were to have a gun in my hand, I might hesitate to pull the trigger; I might not pull it at all. The antidepressant slowly but surely took its effect and I began to ponder if my injury was preventable. *If I had been treated in time with these medications, would I still have jumped?*

Another major change was my appetite. I started to crave snacks in between meals. Instead of asking my parents to kill me, I now asked them to feed me. Wanting to eat was definitely a sign of wanting to live. They bought all kinds of waffles, cookies, and dates to fill my drawer. Eating was my only enjoyment. Food was my most loyal companion. It took my mind away from pain and regret. It never betrayed but always sacrificed. Little did I know that all the deliciousness was as demonic as the fruit Satan gave to Eve. I was blowing up like a balloon.

One morning, I was woken by a horrific scream, "Yvonne, my patient is dead!" The nurse was referring to my elderly roommate. All of a sudden, the siren sounded. Three or four nurses rushed to my room and attempted to resuscitate her. One of the nurses speedily closed the curtain between me and them. My attendant came up to me and held my hands to ease my fear, "This poor lady was puking and having diarrhea all night long. You slept through it all."

Ten minutes later, they gave up on her and announced the time of her death. That was the first time I was near a corpse. Before the nurse could come back to take the body away, I opened up the curtain and had a peek at her. I had never seen a dead body in my life. She was extremely thin and pale. Her skin was dry like the texture of a tree trunk. Her mouth was open. She looked like she was in a bad dream. Death was terrifying and lonely. I felt like I was very far from the place she had gone to. I was certain that I did not want to be where she went. That moment, I realized I no longer wanted to die.

13

After three months in the medical wing, it was time to move on. Under normal circumstances, a spinal cord injured patient would be admitted to a rehab hospital to receive physio and occupational therapy. However, the hospital had concerns about my mental health. I was not ready for rehab yet. Instead, I would be transferred to the most notorious ward of every hospital—the psychiatric ward. My dad had a tour before I moved there. He witnessed two patients who got into a fight; a bunch of lunatics wandering in the hallway and an insane young boy frantically screaming, "Mama! Mama!" My dad told me what he saw and I was frightened. From what I had seen on TV and in movies, mentally ill people were always violent and scary. *Will they beat me up in the middle of the night? Will they eat off my face and limbs?* Despite my protests, I was transferred later that day.

The condition of psychiatry was so much worse compared to other medical wings. The wall was dirty, the hallway was dark, the furniture in the lounge was rugged, the piano was out of tune, the room was small and humid—nothing was right. Most importantly, Irene was gone for good. My attendant services were terminated. I was no longer special. Everyone was crazy in the psychiatric wing. I shared a room with two other girls. There was a tiny window and a noisy air conditioner in our crowded room. In my visual field, I saw nothing but curtains dividing the three of us. I just lay there all day, every day. *Is this hell?* I must have skipped death and gone straight to hell.

The only thing I found comforting was the fact that every nurse was nice and friendly. They were specially bred. Since every patient was physically healthy, they did not have to change diapers, clean up vomit or pack body bags. I was the only patient there who needed extra care. Most of the nurses had to relearn catheterization. They had a big discussion at the end of my bed in regards to where and how to insert a catheter into my lady part.

When my back was strong enough to hold me up, I was given a wheelchair. I'd get up from bed when my parents came to visit. It was nice to have a little mobility by being able to wheel out of the room or even go outside. The first time I got out of my room, I took myself on a full tour around the psychiatric wing. There were three separated sections. The ward where I lived at was designated for adult patients. Fellow loonies spent most of their days strolling back and forth in the corridor. This dark and endless path was a graveyard for hopes and dreams. Every walking dead was trapped inside their own Hades. Some of them were clinically psychotic. They had no soul in their bloodshot eyes. Their humanity was long since gone. The rest of them were sane, but depressed. It seemed impossible to untangle those bitter and sour frowns. Before long, I would be infected with the same strain of zombie virus.

The teenagers were kept apart from the adult patients. Although their rooms and lounge were more furnished, it was equally gloomy and lifeless. There was an alarmed door separating the minors from the adults. Only nurses with an access card could travel freely. I was eighteen at the time. They allowed me to use both sides of the facility.

The third section was an intensive observation unit consisting of four beds. Patients in there were monitored all day long by cameras and two nurses. They were not permitted to leave the small sub-unit. I wondered what kind of people would be locked in there.

One day, as I was sitting in the teen lounge and watching TV, a good-looking young girl was sitting on the couch. She was neatly dressed and her hair was well combed. She had an elegant posture and a lovely manner. I could not help but ask, "Are you a visitor?" By that time, I had willed myself to socialize with other people. "Nope, I am getting a weekend pass. My aunt is taking me out." I wondered what was wrong with her. To me, she looked perfectly well. A few days later, another young girl was in the lounge. She was wearing a hospital gown. Her hair was messy. She had this ill smile on her face and some obvious cuts on her arms. As I looked closely, she was the same girl I saw few days earlier. I felt like I was easier to treat than her.

Another young boy I nicknamed "the Mama Boy". All day long, he'd tirelessly jump up and down and scream "Mama! Mama!" He looked extremely mentally ill. I had seen his mom visiting him. She attempted to tame him and calm him down, but he was strong enough to tackle a bull. Despite his severe mental disability, his mom was patient and loving. One afternoon, Mama Boy ran into the lounge and danced his fingers on the piano. Surprisingly, it was a familiar melody. It was not perfect, but the hoary piano was to blame.

The most interesting patient in the ward was my roommate Julie. There was this horror engraved in her eyes, as if she was constantly reliving a traumatic experience. She always had this crying expression stuck on her face, but there were no tears coming out. She was one of the people that walked in the corridor every day. But unlike other patients, she continued to walk throughout the night. When she got tired, she would sit on the floor to rest for a few minutes before getting up again. I could empathize. During my most acute state, I was not able to sit still. I had to pace back and forth like a caged animal.

My parents were the only parents who would visit their child unconditionally every day. The three of us would sit in the kitchen and have dinner together. My parents would spread the containers across the table. They always brought a meat dish, a seafood dish, a vegetable dish and a hearty soup. That had always been our home's nutritional standard. It was just like before. One of the janitors saw us one day and said, "How lucky you are to have parents like them. A few young children here are abandoned by their parents. There is a Chinese boy who has been here for more than a year. No one ever came to visit him. He lies on his bed all day long. Sometimes he only eats a cheese bar for dinner." I knew whom she was referring to. I remembered seeing an extremely pale and thin Asian boy. His hair was shoulder length. Despite his fragile appearance, he had delicate features. Potentially, he could be a very handsome young man.

One night after my parents left, I was once again tempted by the devil. I found a roll of packing tape in my drawer. It was used during my move to the psychiatric ward. A light bulb went on. I tied my left wrist around the bed rail. I used another big piece to cover my mouth and nostrils. Right away, I could not breathe. That was when I found out how impossible it was to triumph over the feeling of suffocation. My right hand came to rescue with a mind of its own. It quickly ripped the tape off my face. I hated to admit, the first breath of air was incredibly soothing. I gave it another try—it was humanly impossible that I could successfully kill myself like that. I would need help. Julie walked in at that moment. I thought she was too insane to understand what was going on. So I asked her in a very gentle voice, "Hey, Julie sweetheart, can you do me a favor by taping my right hand against the bed rail and putting another piece of tape over my face?" She was puzzled at first, but soon figured me out. "Are you trying to kill yourself? I know how you feel. No, I cannot help you." I underestimated her. "Julie, why are you here?" She was open to share, "I always hear voices. Doctors cannot get rid of my hallucinations. It all started after I was raped by four guys. I can't sleep . . . I was at this other psychiatric hospital; my shoes were stolen." Her threads of conversation would jump from one thought to another. Knowing the trigger of Julie's mental illness, I felt ashamed for what I just did to myself. (Many years later, I met Julie again. She was in a wheelchair due to a failed suicide attempt.)

Surprisingly, my time spent at the psychiatric wing was therapeutic. That dark and hopeless place made me feel like I was not the most unfortunate person in the world.

14

Finally, I was ready to go to Lyndhurst, a rehabilitation hospital for people with spinal cord injuries. It was founded by WWII veterans returning from the war with a serious injury. It was the biggest spinal cord rehabilitation centre in Canada. I was given a spacious private room with a wide window. Dogs of all breeds from nearby neighborhood would walk by my window every day.

I really enjoyed the meals in the cafeteria. Unlike the tasteless food in other hospitals, the ones prepared at Lyndhurst were homemade comfort food served in an all-you-can-eat style. There was once, I ate ten teriyaki chicken drumsticks for supper. Their clam chowder was also a hit. It helped me rediscover the point of living. I was put to bed every evening after dinner. I laid my snacks across the large surface area of my belly, turned on my little TV and flipped through the channels with my greasy fingers. I totally celebrated the lifestyle of a coach potato; *even better*, this potato was lying on an adjustable hospital bed. My favorite junk food was cheese puff. I once ate an entire family pack in one night. My favorite TV show was *Just for Laugh Gags*. I found myself capable of laughing again.

I received one hour of physiotherapy and one hour of occupational therapy every weekday. I would learn all the essential life skills of adapting to using a wheelchair. During our daily session, my physiotherapist Bonnie would stretch me and prevent my joints and muscles from becoming stiff. She was very petite. By this time, I was probably twice her size. Yet, she could toss me like a bowl of salad. My occupational therapist Chandy focused on restoring the strength on my arms and hands. Several months of lying in bed made my upper body so weak that I could not even open up a water bottle. She also took me on an outing to the nearest Tim Hortons. I learned how to order a cup of iced cappuccino and a donut when sitting in a wheelchair. While having our break in the outside world, we were talking about the latest drama inside the Bachelor mansion. For patients under the age of twenty, there was a classroom in the hospital. I was encouraged to spend one hour each day to refresh my Math skills. Joanne was the amazing teacher. She always had this big smile on her face, I mean huge. Her signature smile would brighten up the gloomiest day.

I met a lot of other newly-injured patients coming from all walks of life, no pun intended. We were all coping with the revelation that we would never be able to walk again or poo and pee in a usual way. Some of them had quadriplegia. Having broken their neck meant all four limbs were affected to various degrees. The extreme being they had to control their power wheelchair with their head and chin or by blowing and sucking unto a tube. My parents also connected with other grieving family members. They shared their coping mechanisms and found comfort in each other's company.

Spinal Cord Injury Ontario was on the second floor of the hospital. It is a non-profit organization serving people with spinal cord injury. Rob was one of the peer support coordinators. He came to me one afternoon and signed me up for their membership. Rob was also using a wheelchair. He sat up really straight and moved around with agility and confidence. It was the first time I saw a "cool wheelchair kid" and realized that people with disabilities could also work and be productive in life. A few days after meeting with Rob, my peer match Marilyn came to my room. She was injured in a motorcycle collision many years ago and she had a neck injury as a result. Even though it was the very first time we met, she told me some of her most personal and painful experience in life. Her words were comforting and encouraging, exactly what I needed to hear. Toward the end of the meeting, I cut the cheese. It was silent but deadly and the entire room became a gas chamber, "I am so sorry." I said sheepishly.

Marilyn replied, "That's okay, it's the spinal cord injury, we don't have control over it."

"I'd blame on the high protein diet." We both laughed.

Why is everybody so nice here? It seemed like my injury had snapped me into another world. It opened my eyes to all the tragedies of other people that I would not have known otherwise. It is a world where everyone is so much nicer.

Of course, there were a few exceptions. Remember that South-Asian woman my dad hired when I was at Sunnybrook hospital? Her "treatment" officially began. She'd come with bottles of "holy water" and sugar pills that claimed to have healing power. Before my mother left each day, she would remind me to take those "medications" first thing in the morning. Even though I knew it was a hoax, I took them anyway because they were extremely costly for what they actually were. After a while, I could not stand that witch anymore. One night, I stared right into her eyes and said in a creepy voice, "Do you believe that people who tell lies will be punished inevitably?" I could see a trace of guilt in her eyes. However, my dad ruined the moment by apologizing to her, "I am sorry. My daughter is cuckoo." The other "doctor" was a Chinese acupuncturist. He came to Lyndhurst twice a week to give me acupuncture therapy. Technically, it was my spine that was injured, but my legs and feet were wrongly convicted. He would pinch needles into my lower body and charge them with electricity. A few of my muscle groups would twitch along. My parents were marveled at the sight of my dancing legs. Four thousand dollars were spent in vain before they were finally convinced that spinal nerve damage is impossible to reverse.

Another group of visitors was introduced to me by my dad's coworker Eugene. Eugene was a very devoted Christian. He had no interest in worldly affairs. During lunch time, he would take out his Bible and find a quiet spot to meditate while my dad and his other co-workers were furiously debating over their differences in political views. When Eugene heard about our tragedy, he immediately paid a visit to my parents and prayed for my surgery during that dreadful night. Now that he heard I had come to another hospital where visitations were unrestricted, he was very eager to bring his church people to me. I was overwhelmed seeing all those strangers in my room. Brother Hsieh was among one of the visitors. "My family had gone through a lot of hardships as well. Christ was helping us going through all. You should trust Him as well. You should start praying." I asked, "I am not baptized. Will God listen to my prayer?" He said gently, "If a couple is not married yet, will they still love each other? Being baptized is as symbolic as a piece of paper. You don't have to be baptized to be loved by God. He loves and cares about you unconditionally." That evening, I prayed my very first prayer. It was very amateur, "God help me!"

On the day after, my mother came to Lyndhurst with a serious stomach cramp. She had always been lactose intolerant all her life. She thought the pain had to do with some dairy product she carelessly consumed two days ago. She had been enduring this pain for at least two days! It got so bad on that night that she had to lay on my bed, "I will be fine, just let me rest for a while." My dad insisted of taking her to the Emergency. Fortunately, she got there on time and had her infected appendix removed. She could have died. That was my dad's worst night. He told me that he prayed on that night, it was coincidentally the same plea: "God help me!" Perhaps as a result, my mom had a speedy recovery. For the first time, I felt the humane side of God. That was when I started to pray every day.

15

January 2004

Seven months after my injury, I came home. My parents sold our old place, hoping to rid us of all the negative memories attached to it. Our new condo was brighter and much more spacious. We now lived on the fourteenth floor. I could see the busy city, the whitewashed trees, and the colorful sunset through my window. It took me a while to get used to basic things of such. I felt like I had just returned to civilization after serving a long sentence. I was given a new book to write my life on. What's ahead of me? What was waiting to be written with my sweat and blood? I had no inspiration to compose the table of content and no motivation to brainstorm the blank pages, because once in a while, I still contemplated on the scheme of death.

Seven months of excessive eating made me gain sixty pounds since the day of my injury. The skin on my arms and waist could not cope with such rapid rate of expansion. I got stretch marks all over it. My mom took me to a barber and got me a really short haircut. I looked like a fat boy. My dad hid away my old pictures. He said it was heartbreaking for him to see them. But I still had one in my wallet. I often stared at it for eternity. I reminisced over the ancient days when I stood in front of the mirror and asked mirror-mirror if I was the fairest of all. Now, I never lifted up my head when using the bathroom sink—mirrors were honestly mean. I was careless about what I wore or how I looked. All of my shirts were baggy and cheap. I did not even bother wearing a bra. I simply gave up. I was no longer an arrogant peacock. I was as ugly as a fat toad.

Doing everything on a wheelchair was not easy. All the things I used to do for granted had now become a challenge. The fact that I became so much heavier affected my mobility even more. I needed help with transferring onto the toilet, to the bed; I struggled with putting on clothes and shoes; I had to take strong painkillers to fall asleep at night; I smelled like pee most of the time because of my incontinence. I refused to go out and become a public attraction. I was perfectly fine sentencing myself to house arrest.

When I sat in front of the computer for the first time in months, I was extremely torn. Though I knew I was not going to like what I see, I was tempted to find out how the world had moved on without me. After several attempts, I finally entered the correct password to my email. There were over three hundred unread emails, mostly junks, a few were written by friends around the time of graduation. They wanted to know what happened and where I was. *Well, they probably forgot about me by now.* I was stupid enough to log on to my social network. I went through every body's profile, my friends and my foes. Based on pictures of those killer smiles accompanied by sun-kissed skin, beautiful sceneries, and empty beer bottles, everyone was evidently well; you know, exceptionally well in every single area of their lives. If that wasn't enough, I tortured myself even more by clicking on Will's page. He too, moved on without me. I thought about "us" quite often. To him, it was just a meaningless four weeks; but to me, I would live under his shadow for the rest of my life. "It's not fair! It's not fair!" All at once, sorrows and pain accumulated over the months poured out into rivers of tears. My head started to ache, my heart began to burn. For the next thirty minutes, I was just crying and crying, until I was dizzy and exhausted. That moment, I realized I had just become a prisoner of hate.

16

The only exciting thing about my new life was getting a puppy. We all agreed that we wanted a small dog with a flat nose and a long coat. I learned that a Shih Tzu would match all of our criteria. I looked through the newspaper and found a breeder. The breeder's home was small and smelly. The living conditions there were worse than a shelter. He had over four dogs as his family members and as many as fifteen dogs when they got a new litter. It was at that humble place my little savior was born. When my dad went to pick a puppy, a tiny black and white Shih Tzu stood out from the rest by being extremely energetic and joyful. He jumped up to kiss my dad and immediately made him smile from ear to ear. He was the one. We named him *Heihei*, after a dog we used to own when I was a kid.

My parents were very pleased when they saw how much I adored my new puppy. The fact that I was once again capable of loving something or someone meant I was getting closer to becoming a normal person. This angelic creature was indeed the source of my happiness. He was like my little fluffy tail following me everywhere I went. He was incredibly cute and smart. Within weeks, he learned a lot of tricks and demonstrated his potential as a circus performer. Being an extreme glutton, he'd trade his soul for food. Oh yes, he had a soul. He conveyed all his emotions and thoughts with his black-diamond eyes. He understood all the complexities of humanity—just like a human trapped in a dog's body. I never wanted to place him down on the floor. He literally grew up on my lap.

My best friend Teresa had moved to London, Ontario. We almost lost in touch at this point. The two friends I wanted to invite back to my life were Linda and Sherry. We were really close in high school. Not long after I returned home, they took me to Scarborough Town Centre. In my previous life, I used to shop at this mall all the time. I would dress up in my prettiest garments and count on the attention from fellow shoppers. This time, however, was different. It was my first time going to a populated place in a wheelchair. I was surrounded by fashion elites and gabby teenagers. I had absolutely no interest in shopping. Instead, I was busy with my self-consciousness. I felt like I was the center of unwanted attentions. Children surveyed me with their blunt curiosity. Women looked down on me with seeming superiority. Men looked right through me as if I was transparent. In the eyes of the equally weak and disabled I saw a mirror image of myself. Linda and Sherry took turns pushing me around. I felt embarrassed for my friends. I brought down their status.

When the day ended, Sherry gave me a letter and asked me to read it later. When I got home, I opened the envelope and saw a beautifully written note ". . . Do not feel discouraged about what happened. There is nothing to be ashamed of. Be strong and brave . . ." I don't think I appreciated the note as much as I should.

A few weeks later, two acquaintances sent me a message via MSN. They heard about what had happened to me and wanted a confirmation from me. I was upset knowing how many people might have learned about my failed suicide attempt. I asked them who that little bird was. Both of them told me it was Linda. I was furious. Immediately I sent her a message and told her off. Linda is the best kind of friend a person could ever ask for, but you do not want to be sassy Linda's enemy. Understandably, she did not react well to my comment. That was the end of our friendship. Before long, I lost Sherry due to another ridiculous accusation. I soon found myself being a complete loner. I felt like no one would ever befriend me and take me seriously.

One day, Heihei climbed onto the edge of my window. The only thing that separated him and the forty-meter fall was the thin window screen. I almost jumped out of my wheelchair to scoop him into my embrace. I sank my face into his coat and cried hysterically, "You are the only friend I have. I cannot lose you!"

17

September 2004

The first chapter of my new life began as I was about to enter University of Toronto as a first year student. I was intimidated. My parents wanted me to take a 40 percent course load. Unlike other Chinese parents, they had very low expectations for me, "Passing is enough."

School was very difficult in the beginning. I was haunted by people from my previous life. For some of them, I was too disfigured to be recognized. But for the ones who were once my "friends", I felt like they were avoiding me like a plague. I was extremely jealous of my colleagues. Everyone was either in love or in search of love. They all seemed to belong to an entourage. Their laughter and playful screams sounded intolerably perky to my ears. The knowledge of them partying and lusting reminded me of the day when I turned eighteen and excitedly accepted my entitlement of vigor and rebellion. But unfortunately, I never got the chance to exercise my privilege. In this vibrant and dynamic campus, I was the only person living a lame life, quite literally. A few people were nice to me in class, but I did not want to friend anybody. I did not want anyone to feel comfortable enough to ask me about my past and why am I using a wheelchair. I told myself my only reason of going to school was learning.

The lack of social life in school made me focus on studying. However, my poor mental health affected my concentration and cognition. I had to work extra hard. Sometimes, I had to retype virtually the entire chapter to enhance my memory or record a lecture to listen to it over and over again. Besides eating, sleeping, and doing exercise, I was studying all the time. My dog would sleep right next to my workstation. After he woke up from a nap, he would nudge me and want to climb onto my lap, as if he was reminding me to take a break. When I held this live stuffed animal in my arms, I was a kid again.

When I received my first year's grade, I realized they had a therapeutic effect on me. For the first time in a long time, I felt a sense of accomplishment, and maybe a whiff of hope.

In my second year, I took an interesting course called abnormal psychology. It teaches about different types of mental illness and other mental health related issues. It was a course that helped me gain a lot of insights into my own condition. I realized that I was born with a strong genetic predisposition toward depression, which could explain all the phobias and neurotic behaviors I displayed even when I was a child. By its nature, depression is a medical condition and medication is the key to recovery. Had I had enough such knowledge at the time, I probably would not have taken that fateful jump. This realization made me want to share my story. But I was afraid that people would judge me after knowing the truth about my injury. I was already burdened by the stigma of having a physical disability, would I be strong enough to be known as someone who is also mentally ill? I prayed about it.

On the day when we were about to have a lecture on mood disorder, I went to Professor Zakzanis's office one hour before the class began. I said, "I have a story to share. I wonder if I can give a speech about depression based on personal experience." I caught him by surprise. I was going to give him a long explanation and a preview of what I was about to say. But instead, he said, "sure, I will meet you in the classroom. I will give you five extra credits at the end of the term."

"I rather have a reference letter." I bargained.

"I will give you both."

With Professor Zakzanis's blessing, I talked in front of five hundred fellow students about what happened to me, the desperateness, the despair, and the dilemma of a suicide. I was able to give people an understanding of depression that no textbooks could cover. My English had never been that fluent. I had never been that gifted as a public speaker. As it turned out, it was phenomenal! Many people were in tears while listening to me. Afterwards, I received over fifty "fan mails". A few people told me that they too were going through tough times and they decided to seek treatment after believing that depression is treatable. The Professor was very impressed. That was a huge turning point. I never thought I could turn such negative experience into good use. I never thought anything positive could ever come out of my loss.

My world changed. I felt like strangers began to smile at me in the hallway and more people were willing to hold the doors for me. School was not as dreadful as before. By the end of the semester, I even had two friends—Wendy and Grace. We went to the same high school together, but at the time we were only acquaintances. I thought they were too nerdy to hang out with. But as we got reconnected in University, I realized they were still the same—pure, simple, and hardworking. They never wore make-up, never gossiped, and never dropped the F-bomb. To me, they had the most beautiful souls in the whole entire universe.

There were other positive changes. Physically, my left leg became much stronger. I regained a lot of control in my left thigh. The muscle groups were visibly contracting. My right leg was more paralyzed with obvious atrophies. But amazingly, with the support of leg braces, I was able to walk very slowly with a walker. I'd practice walking in the corridor of our condo building every single day while my mom pushed my wheelchair slowly behind me. When I sat down to rest, she would pass me my water bottle and wipe the sweat off my forehead. She pampered me each time as though I had just finished a round of a boxing match. Gradually, I lost twenty pounds by being careful with my diet and sticking to my exercise routine. Spiritually, I found myself increasingly hungry for God's Words. I'd watch the *700 Clubs* and read my *Daily Bread* devotion each day. We'd also meet with Eugene's group on Saturday night and attend church on Sunday morning. God's teaching was always timely and necessary.

I was doing well, really well. Some days, I was even happy, *quite amazing.*

18

April 2006

Out of the blue, I began to have insomnia again. Like the first time, I had this overflowing amount of mental energy that kept me thinking and talking all day long. But different from the first time, I was not depressed. I had no explanation as to why I fell ill again. After seven sleepless nights and days, I returned to the psychiatric ward in Sunnybrook hospital. During my stay, my symptoms became increasingly psychotic. I would stay up all night screaming, flailing, and shouting. I had no inhibitions in my actions and words. I was rude to everybody. I spat on the floor, threw pillows everywhere and called my nurses "bitches and hoes". I even stole food in the fridge that belonged to other patients and once binged ate for two hours. After observing me, my psychiatrist Dr. McCullagh told my parents that I was clinically manic. He diagnosed me with bipolar disorder. "Bipolar is what she had all along. It's common that bipolar patients are misdiagnosed for clinical depression. Most likely, she had mania before her first episode of depression in 2003, but we couldn't have known it. And because she was on the wrong medication over the years, her illness came back again." Dr. McCullagh paused, then with a lighter tone he said, "Give her about three weeks, she will come back to herself." Right away, I was placed on Lithium, which is the predominant treatment for bipolar disorder.

During those three weeks, I continued to go nuts. I had a lot of delusions and hallucinations. I imagined myself being able to communicate with God by searching for His messages in the stars and the clouds. A little bit of biblical inspiration turned me into a "healer". I would approach other patients and lay my hand on them like the way I read about how Jesus cured the incurables. Everyone was equally tuned out of reality. Some of them were so obedient. They would extend their arms and close their eyes as I performed "miracles". I kept on imagining that there was a big party taking place outside of the hospital, but I was locked up in this loony bin. There was a sign above the fire alarm that said, "Doors will be opened once the alarm sounds." In order to escape, I pulled the alarm. Sirens began to sound across the entire hospital. Fire trucks immediately came to the rescue. It cost the hospital five thousand dollars to reset the alarm. Two days later, I pulled the alarm yet again . . . As a result, I got locked up in the intensive observation unit—I now learned whom it was for. The sub-confinement was so small that I barely had space to turn my wheelchair. On that night, I still managed to throw a private party in my head with all of my imaginary friends. The next morning, my parents saw that all of my clothes and covers were torn. I was lying on my stomach, limbs spreading in all directions and butt naked . . . My dad stormed out into the corridor and instantly turned into one of "us". He blended in perfectly with the other patients, wandering and stumbling on the boulevard with his broken dreams. While pacing back and forth, he was thinking hard about what he had done in the past that rendered him this punishment. This time, he was counting his sins.

As Dr. McCullagh predicted, three weeks later, I no longer acted like a barbarian. From one extreme to the other, I was aloof and stagnant most of the day. I felt like my brain had been traumatized. It was very difficult to fall asleep and stay asleep. By morning, I did not feel like getting up at all. Dr. McCullagh explained, "It's typical that depression always follows mania. It is a signature characteristic of this disorder . . ." *Oh man, not again.*

After another two weeks, I was discharged from the hospital. I attempted to return to school. I had just finished my midterm exams before my hospitalization. My marks were good, but very quickly, I found it impossible to pick up where I had left off. I failed to keep up with the demands of my courses with my impaired cognitive abilities. I was unable to comprehend anything I read. I had no choice but to drop all my three courses. On top of that, summer school was going to start in July, it did not seem like I could recover in time. With a pace like this, it would take a decade to get my degree. I was totally devastated.

Boredom and loneliness started to consume me. I had no interest in anything. I tried to read, but I found it hard to concentrate. Before the sentence ended, I had already forgotten what the beginning was about. I did not want to watch TV. Seeing people kissing, making love, and nurturing a family was a painful reminder that I would most likely die alone. Twice a day, I practiced walking in my condo's hallway that felt like an overheated oven. Though each pointless step always led back to the origin, it was still the most productive routine of my day. As for the rest of the day, I merely indulged in endless regrets and self-pity. I'd fantasize about reversing that fateful jump. In my mental picture, I tried to reconstruct that morning. I imagined myself going out to the balcony, inhaling the fresh air and being cured by the Healer's breath. But every time I opened my eyes again, my damn wheelchair traveled me back to the cruelty of reality.

Food once again became my only source of comfort. Within a month, I regained all the weight I had lost. I was eating like calories had no its lethal effects on me. Diet drinks were replaced by their full-fat version. Chocolates and candies were consumed religiously as if they were vitamin supplements. I forced my mom to take me to a buffet for at least once a week. And more than occasionally, I would warm myself a beef patty and a can of soup right before bedtime. I never refrained from opening my bloody mouth when even a hint of hunger arose to woo me. My weight quickly soared toward 200lbs while my self-esteem plunged to below freezing point.

Aside from that, I experienced a lot of side effects to my new medication. I developed acne all over my face. Not an inch of my skin was given mercy. Unlike ordinary breakouts I used to get as a teen, this type of acne wormed very deep into my skin. It refused to go away, and when it finally did, my face was left with permanent scars and discolorations. I freaked a dozen of kids off in public. At one point, it was so bad that I wished I could veil myself with a burqa. In addition, I began to develop a strange bowel condition. I would be constipated for five to seven days, and then all of a sudden, I would have a severe diarrhea that emptied everything in my system. The week following the dramatic bowel movement, I would jam up again. The cycle went on and on.

The thing that bothered me the most was my poor quality of sleep. I was counting on it to take away one third of my pathetic life, yet it was tremendously difficult to fall asleep. Each night, my mom would sit beside my bed and read me a "bed time story" with an extremely soft and hypnotic voice. It had the effect of a lullaby and that was the only way I would feel drowsy.

On one gorgeous summer day, I could not find a single reason to go outdoors. I felt more secure inside my jail cell. I sat beside my window and looked downward. While listening to the laughter of kids playing in the pool and staring at that invisible rainbow crowning above them, my heart was bleeding envy. I wished I could supernaturally become one of those kids. But if being a happy human was too much to ask for, I wished I could become a rich person's pet, like Paris Hilton's Chihuahua that owned a fancy wardrobe and a Barbie mansion. I was even jealous of my own dog. How I wish my happiness could be so easily satisfied as when flakes of food got swept off the table. But as for me . . . nothing could lift up the corners of my lips; my depression had stripped away all the colors in my world and pushed me into a gray zone.

At the end of that thought, I looked down toward the ground floor, fourteen stories from where I was. I knew if I were to transfer my body onto the edge of the window and shift just a few inches out, death would swallow my misery for good. The only thing that separated me from falling for this temptation was a thin window screen. As I was touching it and entertaining the idea of cutting it open, I suddenly saw my parents' weary faces. I thought about them. I thought about all their tears, brokenness, and sacrifices over the years and I was torn, a devil and an angel poofed onto my opposite shoulders. Then, I remembered an incident that happened a year prior to that . . .

One day, my mom and I were shopping at Scarborough Town Centre. As we were strolling toward the food court, I felt a tap on my shoulder. I turned around and saw a middle-aged man. He was wearing a poncho looking like an Indian or perhaps a Mexican. *He's probably asking for direction or time* was my first guess. But instead, he said plainly, "Jesus will bless you." Strangers told me that all the time as a way of expressing their sympathy, but somehow, this man gave me a chill. "Jesus will bless me?" I wanted to confirm if this was really what he said. He nodded, turned around and walked away in opposite direction. "What was that?" Even my mom thought it was strange.

At that moment when I was once again allured by death I saw that strange man's face. "Jesus will bless you. Jesus will bless you . . ." His voice was echoing in my head, loud enough to convince me of its validity. It forced me to believe that this was not the end for me. It forced me to stay patient in suffering. I wheeled away from the window . . .

December 31, 2006. I went to bed early. I had nowhere to celebrate the first bell of the New Year. I had no idea how I would survive the dreadful night, the pending torture of another year, and the bitterness of all the years to come. The shouts of the countdown followed by screams of ecstasy leaked from my neighbour's land to engulf me in a sea of loneliness. The year had advanced, my soul aged along with it.

I held my Bible like a Teddy Bear while praying earnestly. Although God's presence was no longer felt, I forced myself to believe. After all, He's my only hope. I needed that first prayer of the year to fuel my diminishing faith. "Save me, Lord, I have no idea how, I don't know in what way my life will become better. But, Lord, You know the way. Save me."

19

February 2007

One day I saw an article that talked about online dating for people with disabilities and a website called *DisabledDating.com*. The idea was appealing to me. Maybe a friend or a companion would become the antagonist of my depression. I picked a picture of my seventeen-year-old self and uploaded it onto my profile. I put "paraplegia" as my type of disability and in the "about me" section, I wrote, "Looking for a glimpse of heaven." I was amazed about how many potential matches I found within my area. Some of the guys were cute. I wondered if they cheated on their pictures as well. That day, I ordered anti-acne product over the Internet. I suddenly felt like I wanted to look pretty again.

Before long, I got messages from suitors all around the world. They all seemed to be very desperate. It was fun chatting with them. It occurred to me that I was less preoccupied with problems in real life and more indulged in my virtual reality. Besides studying and exercising, most of my time was spent on the Internet and fishing for anything that swam toward me. Though those connections were superficial and mostly meaningless, I was hooked. Then one day, it actually happened. A ship by the name of Aaron sailed into my remote and deserted harbor.

His choice of profile picture was modest. He listed "visual impairment" as his disability. We exchanged MSN and started chatting. I learned that he lived in Chicago, and had a degree in Law. His father was Spanish and his mother belonged to an ethnic minority group in China. Aaron was born in China and moved to America when he was about eight years old. Therefore, he spoke perfect Mandarin. His love for Chinese culture and food was profound. Aaron said he had a condition called juvenile cataract. He used to be completely blind as a child. After receiving a surgery at ten, his vision got better. But he was still visually impaired. I was relieved knowing that he too lives with a flaw—a perfect imperfection.

For the first time in a very long time, I was looking forward to getting up from bed each morning. The thought of talking to Aaron gave me power to fuel the day. Things happening in my immediate surroundings bothered me no more. The core of my happiness was a person on the other side of the computer screen, inches away from my fingers, yet as distant as a dream—finally, I was entitled to dream again.

At the two-month point, Aaron expressed his desire to come to Toronto. "I am coming in April! How exciting is that? I have borrowed a travel guide from the library and I am reading about Toronto." The affection was miraculously mutual! But, I was suddenly caught in a dilemma. On one hand, I was delirious knowing that he wanted to take our "relationship" to the next level. I had no doubt that he would be my ultimate cure. But on the other hand, I was scared of meeting him in person. At this time, Aaron still thought that my profile picture was up to date. What if he were to be confronted by the truth, would he take back everything he had given me so far? I was once again enveloped by this familiar feeling of fear and depression. I would rather our relationship never progress and live eternally in this illusion of love. Then, I thought about his visual impairment. Maybe the mist in his eyes would mask my acne, and maybe the outline of my body would only be a blur to him. I prayed that Aaron would be too blind to see.

I was determined to transform myself. I began to eat healthier and exercise more vigorously. Food was no longer my comforter. It had become my foe. I cut all my snacks and sweet drinks. The acne treatment actually worked, I noticed some obvious improvement on my skin. Though I still had a lot of discolorations, I managed to cover them with makeup. I put away all of my old clothes and bought a new wardrobe. But unfortunately, a few weeks of "boot camp" were too short to grow my hair longer or lose ten inches off my waist line. Nonetheless, I was told that my smile made me much prettier.

20

Aaron came as promised. He stayed at a friend's house during his visit in Toronto. When he opened the door for me, there was a moment of awkwardness. We rigidly shook hands before I entered the room. He's at least six feet tall with no definitive Asian features. He wore a pair of dark framed glasses, looking a bit like a grown-up Harry Potter. However, to my surprise, he was nothing like someone with a visual impairment. Not only did his eyes looked bright and focused, he was navigating the room without any difficulties. *Was his vision really that bad after all?*

We started to chat in Chinese. He did most of the talking while I was pondering in my mind as to why a beauty like him would bother to come all the way from Chicago to meet a beast like me. I did not have much to say. After years of being socially inactive, I had lost touch with the world. I knew very little about the latest fad and the coolest trend. I simply nodded and smiled as my ways of contributing to the conversation. Our first meeting was defined as very "friendly". I thought it was only a bit better than a blind date gone south. I left his place thinking this would be the end of us. From that point on, I would treat him as a friend and take him sightseeing during the rest of the week—lest his airfare spent in vain.

The next day, Aaron took the bus to my home. He was well dressed, looking more handsome and mature in the bright day light.

Upon his suggestion, we went to The Hockey Hall of Fame. I was never a sports fan; I knew nothing about hockey. Aaron on the other hand, had been playing hockey since he was a child. He was fascinated by memorabilia of legendary players and famous events in hockey history. Several times, he asked strangers to take pictures for us. He'd kneel down beside my chair to accommodate my height. He really wanted me to be part of his meaningful experience. In the midst of our tour, there was a mini hockey rink and people were lining up to shoot pucks. Aaron's eyes glowed. When it was his turn to show off, he had a perfect score. I was more and more confused by the fact that he appeared to possess normal vision.

We found a spot in the food court during lunch. One topic led to another, he started to talk about his past relationships. He said that he used to date a girl who also had a disability. They had been together for two years. But at the time, he did not want to settle down just yet. Then all of a sudden, he caught me off guard by saying, "Well, now I have you." I almost got choked by a chunk of my burger. It was surreal. I thought I had misheard him. *Was that a hallucination? Did I skip my medication last night? He still wanted to be with me after seeing the real me?* Either he really did have an impaired vision, or he had an impaired taste.

On the third day, Aaron came to my home early in the morning and took me to the Shoe Museum. He read about it in the tourist guide. Living in Toronto for almost a decade, I had barely done anything fun in the city. I had never heard about this famous attraction. He took me to the museum by subway. I had not taken the subway since being in a wheelchair. I was too afraid to explore outside of my comfort zone, but Aaron gave me his protection. I felt safe and brave beside him. There was no need for me to figure out which stop to get off. Aaron knew the route and each transfer point as if he had been a Torontonian all his life.

That evening, we went to the best Japanese restaurant in my area. Up till this point, our conversation remained "friendly". We had not officially talked about "us". I had no idea where and how this would go on. I was totally powerless. My fate was in Aaron's merciful hands. When we finished eating and came out from the dining area,

I bumped into someone who had long since died in my heart. Believe it or not, it was Will! He and his girlfriend were waiting to be seated. *Fate is equally bitchy.* Immediately he recognized me. His face turned pale, his lips were trembling, and the muscles on his cheeks began to twitch. He pulled his cap all the way down to cover his face. His girl-friend noticed him behaving strangely. She alternated puzzling looks between me and him. I was awestruck. I did not know how to react. I had not thought about him for a long while and I had never thought about how my injury might have affected him. I always painted him as a cold-blooded serpent, but quite contrary . . . it looked like he had borne a great burden of guilt over the years. Had his life been changed in ways he had no control over? All of a sudden, I forgave him.

Aaron was completely oblivious of the situation. He was trying to figure out how to get me out of the restaurant. There was one step at the exit. Finally, he waved at me and signaled me to move toward the door. I decided to move on and move toward Aaron, my future. Aaron used his body to block the door from being shut, by using only one hand he effortlessly pulled my wheelchair down that step. While we were strolling on the sidewalk right outside the restaurant, Aaron suddenly rested his hand on my back, an intimate gesture that defined our relationship to me and to the world. All of a sudden, I felt like I was forgiven.

On Aaron's last day in Toronto, we invited him to dine at my home. My parents spoiled him with all the dishes they were good at making. The two men were drinking beers and talking about China. My dad could not have been happier. With great excitement, he said, "Let's take a road trip to New York City! We need a vacation after all these years!" Right away, Aaron said, "I want to come too. I will fly back to Chicago first and meet you in New York!"

Our three-day trip to New York was very memorable. We went to the most famous museums and attractions in the city. Everywhere we went, Aaron always put his arms around me and shamelessly paraded our love. People stared at us with curiosity and confusion. I was very self-conscious. My demon told me that these people thought I was unworthy of a boyfriend like him. I was not dateable. That's why I was more willing to stay in the hotel room with Aaron. It was like a honeymoon, but I made clear that I did not want to have intimacy before marriage. He respected me and made me to know that he was more than satisfied with just kisses. For hours, we pressed together in bed while being separated by our full garment. He repressed his sexuality by expressing it in words. He said with passion that I was a beautiful woman and he was lucky to have me. In fact, he repeated it for so many times that I started to doubt if he really saw the world like everyone else. Perhaps he perceived angles and shades with a different mechanism; perhaps colors and shapes had a twisted formation in his eyes; perhaps he was not even human. For some reason, no matter how hard I tried to loosen myself in his caresses, it was impossible to let go that feeling of fear. In my head, I endlessly asked myself, *why would he love me? What's loveable about me? Is it because my disability evokes his pity? Is he a superhero who saves desperate disabled girls?* Besides contemplating those unsearchable answers, I was constantly haunted by the strong possibility of incontinence or not being able to control my gas . . .

On the morning of our last day together, he asked me to show him my surgical scar. I lifted up the back of my shirt and exposed the long scar along my broken spinal column. I had never seen it myself. He ran his fingers along the bumps and pits before saying, "Without it, you are perfect."

Before we bid farewell, he promised he would do his best to meet again. I left New York feeling like Aaron had taken most of me with him, my mind, my heart, and my soul. On the road, I was hoping that I could die happily in a car collision. I hoped I would never see the day when Aaron says he loves me no more. I hoped I could close my eyes for good before his eyes were finally opened.

21

W e came safely back to Toronto.

Aaron said he was researching on how to practice law in Canada. It turned out that he would have to go back to school and redo the whole thing all over again. *That sucks.* Then one day, he called with great excitement, "I got a job offer from a law firm in China. I am going to work there as a consultant!" He always wanted to work and live in China. It was a big deal for him, but my heart sank a little bit. This meant that more distance would be added onto our already-long-distance relationship. I suddenly wanted to go back with him, but I knew it would not be realistic.

In the shortest amount of time possible, Aaron moved to China. He quickly adapted to his new life. He became popular as a charming foreigner that speaks fluent Mandarin. Because of the difference in time zone, we could not live chat anymore. Instead, we began to use e-mail. We'd write at least three times a week. We talked about our life, what was new and exciting. But without having him being part of the experience, it took a lot of effort to describe events and people in plain text. I had to think very hard about what to write. Sometimes, I even made up interesting stories to give the impression that I had a fun life.

In reality, I had no life. Since I had come back from New York, I began to diet and exercise like a Biggest-Loser contestant. The raw fibers in my sugarless chows were absolute delights. Due to strict portion control, I fell asleep every night in the grumbling noise of my godforsaken stomach. Aside from walking and riding my stationary bike, I wanted to learn how to swim again. Everyone in this world is either a sinker or a floater and I am the latter with impressive buoyancy. Within two days, I conquered the fear of drowning and was able to paddle in the water with my arms while dragging my legs along. Before long, I was comfortable enough to swim independently. Slowly and gradually, I mastered the breaststroke, backstroke, and freestyle. I'd swim for at least forty-five minutes each day. Three months later, I lost more than 40lbs and could almost qualify as "curvy". For the first time since my injury, I saw a familiar stranger in the mirror. I also got a tattoo on my back. It was a drawing of two roses winding along a thorn branch. It strategically covered up the surgical scar. But the bad news was my acne had returned. The right side of my face was worse than the left side. It was all because of a side effect of Lithium. I coped by concealing it under makeup. Dr. McCullagh decided to put me on another medication called Epival; hopefully it would be more effective in treating my illness with minimal side effects.

During those same months, Aaron and I parted further and faster than I had expected. Not only did he write less and less, but the length of his email was getting shorter and shorter. Our occasional phone conversations often ended in silence and awkwardness. It occurred to me that our love was built on a very shallow foundation that could not withstand the destruction of time and distance.

Out of the blue, my parents suggested we should go back to China to visit my relatives for the first time in nine years. We would go to Hong Kong first to meet up with Aaron. He sounded like he was looking forward to seeing me again and even suggested to go to Fuzhou with me to meet the rest of my family. I was pleasantly surprised. I reproached myself for doubting him. *Perhaps he was just busy with his job at the law firm.*

After four months, Aaron and I met again in Hong Kong. Unlike in the movies, we did not celebrate our reunion with juicy and zesty passion. We simply sat there and talked. *Correction*, it was more like I listened to him talk while trying really hard on thinking about what to say and how to say them. *Is this interesting? Does that sound stupid?* The harder I tried the bigger the lump that jammed up in my throat. It was as if someone pressed the mute button on me. *Oh boy, was I boring as hell.*

"So I just finished talking about my life. What about yours?" Aaron asked.

"Hmm . . . Nothing much was going on. Oh, I am going to show you my tattoo." I lifted up the back of my shirt and proudly showed off my tattoo. In a way, the scar was gone. Did that make me perfect in his eyes?

"Oh, nice." He did not comment any further.

Even though I looked thinner and prettier compared to the first time we met, Aaron had become colder. When we were in public, he no longer wanted to wrap his arms around me. While we rode in the tour bus, he was always on the phone, texting and calling. On our ferry to Macau, he took out a book to read during what could have been a romantic sail. I intentionally sat on his right side and presented him with my less-acne-prone cheek. I fixed my gaze on him in the hope that he would lift his eyes to meet mine, but he failed to acknowledge my desperate desire for his attention. Then, it hit me— Aaron was blind, but now he sees.

Before we flew to Fuzhou, Aaron said he would come a week later. I did not think he was serious. Why would he waste money and time on someone he no longer likes? Once again, my sunshine was gone; I was dyed in blues from head to toe.

My dad had a big family consisting of over twenty people. All my relatives gathered at my grandpa's house to wait for our arrival. My relatives rejoiced upon seeing me for the first time in nine years. I could read them somehow. Behind their big smiles, there was sorrow. I was no longer the little girl they knew when I left China. I did not return in triumph. My grandpa was the only one who utterly displayed his heartache. His eyes glassed over and for a whole minute, he struggled to find the appropriate words, "It's good that you are back." My dad is his youngest son. I am his only granddaughter. Somehow, his love for us made him believe that I would be the most successful grandchild among all my cousins. Yet, I disappointed him.

One of my friends from grade seven happened to know my grandpa. She learned about my return and told all of my other friends from junior high school. They decided to come visit me. Everyone took a step back as they saw me and my wheelchair, in speechless awe they stood. I put up a fake smile and kicked in my actress instinct. I told them a story I had rehearsed several times the day before, "Let me tell you how freaky the car accident was . . ." In grade seven I was the president of the class, the queen bee of my hive. I used to lead my bitches in every social function. We loved and *loved* to gossip over who is cute and who is ugly, who likes whom and whose virginity might have been taken by whom. *Alas,* these girls reminded me so much of my short period of glory when I was a notorious adolescent . . . But now, hearing my friends talking about how life had been treating them over the years, I felt like I was definitely at the bottom of this social stratum.

I spent the first week touring my hometown. The city had been transformed by modernity. I hardly recognized the neighborhood where I grew up. Although China had been keeping abreast with developed countries, city planners had no concept of wheelchair accessibility in mind. It was hard for me to navigate on the bumpy and stony pedestrian path. I had no choice but to share lanes with the bicyclists. People would bluntly fix their gazes on me until their visual field could no longer contain me. Most of them were just curious. They had rarely seen people with disabilities in public. A few of them even came up to me and commented on my fancy wheelchair. They wanted to know where they could buy one for their relatives. "It's made in Canada. I live in Canada." "Wow, lucky you!" Sometimes, you really need someone else to remind you to count your blessings.

One day, I decided to catch up on my emails. As soon as I logged on, my MSN window popped up. It was Aaron! "Hey, I have been trying to contact you. I realize I don't have a number to reach you. I am boarding my plane this afternoon!" I was dumbfounded. I had not bothered to give Aaron my grandpa's number because I never thought he would actually come. "Oh! What time is your flight? I will pick you up."

Four hours later, Aaron was sitting beside me and being extremely chatty. "Thank God I finally got hold of you. I asked my brother how would I be able to find you if I were to go to Fuzhou without knowing anybody. He said I should go anyway and wait for you to call me. I am so glad that it worked out. Phew, that was close." *Unbelievable.*

We drove Aaron to one of the top hotels in the city. When we were left alone in his room, our initial excitement began to fade. We quickly ran out of things to say and found ourselves enveloped in eerie silence. I beefed up, leaned close to him, and kissed him. I wanted to relive our times in New York. I wanted to revive his feeling for me, Aaron reciprocated. At that moment, if he asked me to give him my virginity, I would offer myself wholeheartedly, and if I could chain him to me with his child, I would gladly sacrifice my first born on the altar, but he had no intention to unwrap me.

To everyone's surprise, I brought a boyfriend home. My relatives tried to interact with this interesting stranger, but there was not much they shared in common. Aaron stayed by my side during every family gathering. He was quiet and always wearing a polite smile. My oldest aunt noticed the estranged aura between us. She shielded her mouth with one hand and said to my dad in a low voice, "I am not very optimistic about it."

A week later, Aaron had to fly back to Shenzhen. We bid farewell at the airport. He kissed me lightly on the lip. "Zai Jian!" It literally means "see you again" in Chinese. He turned around, shook hands with my parents and my two relatives, then, picked up his luggage and began walking toward the gates. He did not turn back to spare me another glance. As he disappeared into the crowd, I was positive that I would never see him again. I asked myself, "Am I prepared for this inevitable breakup? Will I fall into another depression?" *Oh, Lord, this time I have You, this time should be different . . .*

22

Two weeks after I returned to Canada, our relationship ended.

The trauma of the past came back to haunt my parents. They were secretly observing my sleep and monitoring me for any signs of my ill-being. To my surprise, I did not suffer from insomnia or any clinical symptoms of depression. Instead, I'd look forward to sleeping, because it was a time for restoration and healing. When I woke up in the morning, I felt refreshed and my heartache was duller than the day before.

Cultural norm suggested that I should look for a rebound. I logged back on to that website where I met Aaron. But before long, I realized my happiness no longer depended on another person's provision. I was self-sufficient. I was doing well, really well to a point where I was confused. I even asked myself, *Is this normal that I am not suffering?*

One day, a revelation hit me. The new medication had taken its effect. Not only had my acne stopped popping out, but the quality of my sleep became much better. I had never experienced my inner state with such peace and contentment. Being a human felt differently compared to ever before! It was like being asleep for over a century and when I suddenly woke up, the world was astonishingly beautiful and brand new to me.

By the beginning of 2008, I had totally recovered from that breakup. I never held grudges against Aaron. In fact, he would always be special in my heart. I believed God sent him to save me. My love for him had transformed myself. I carried on my healthy life style, only this time I was doing it for me. Neighbors who had not seen me for a while could hardly recognize me, "Nancy! I could only tell it was you by your voice! What a miracle!" *Miracle Indeed.*

My life officially started at the age of twenty-three.

EPILOGUE

Now

I never looked back since the day I woke up. In 2011, I graduated from University of Toronto with a Bachelor of Science degree specializing in human psychology. I soon found a job at Spinal Cord Injury Ontario, located inside Lyndhurst rehab hospital. Being a former patient, I was able to help people cope with their injury and adapt to their new life. In 2014, I was in a live theater production called Borne directed by the amazing Judith Thompson. All of the nine cast members were people with physical disabilities. We acted out our stories in twenty-four sold-out performances. It made a great impact on the audience as they learned the strength and resilience of the human spirit.

I continue to speak to Professor Zakzanis's class each year and I also speak to high school students each week in the hopes of preventing injuries, raising awareness about mental health issues, and reducing stigmas against people with disabilities. I am also on the board of directors of a charity called the Tamara Gordon Foundation, which gives scholarships and moral support to postsecondary students living with physical disabilities.

In the past seven years, my parents and I travelled all around the world to breathtaking places like Banff, Hawaii, Rome, and

Paris. Shamelessly speaking, we still live happily together. I made so many friends along the way. I have a squad of BFFs who share common faith and interests with me; they have always been there for me through all the ups and downs . . . Oh yes, I will always believe in love, the kind of love that's above reason and beyond logic. Perhaps I have to wait a life time for my match in heaven to appear; perhaps he will show up as I turn at the next intersection.

I used to regret about that fateful jump. I used to think that I would always live with that regret for the rest of my life. But over the years, good things and good people crossed my path because my life's trajectory had been completely changed by that jump. I now think that this whole experience is an absolute blessing in disguise. It helps me gain things that surpass the physical ability to walk—I became strong and brave; I learned about forgiveness and patience; I witnessed unconditional love and sacrifice; and most importantly, I met my Savior Jesus Christ. I finally knew the meaning of that rugged Cross and its saving grace on wretches like me.

On my ten-year anniversary, I revisited our old condo. As I saw how lofty the eighth floor was compared to that humble pile of soil, I realized I fell onto God's soft and solid palm. *Father, thank you for taking that leap with me.*

5-month old

4 years old

2 month before injury

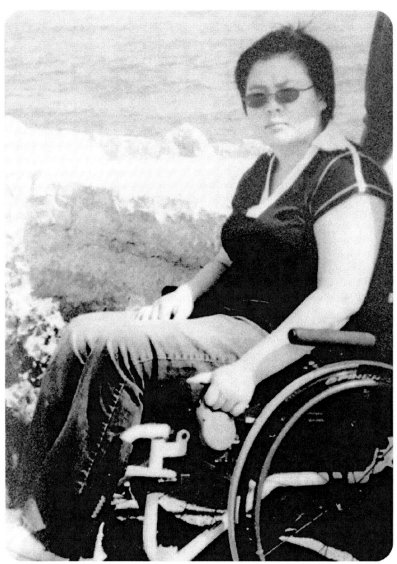

1 year post injury

Heihei visiting me when I was in the hospital again in 2006

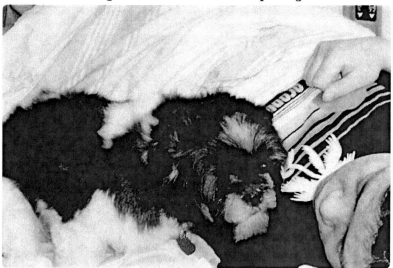

Graduation Day, 2011

our life now

Performing Borne with my fellow cast: Dan Harvey, Dan Raralio, David Shannon, Harley Nott, Joshua Dvorkin, Maayan Ziv, Nikoletta Erdelyi, and Russell Winkelaar

SMILE :)

What Do I Know about Mental Illness

Over the years, I tried to gain as much knowledge as possible about my condition. I truly feel like if I knew then what I know now about mental illness, things would be so different. Right now, I want to share my insights into this topic. (Please note that this is based on my experience and reading about mental illness. It might not be completely agreed upon by every health care professional.)

My Early Signs of Mental Illness

When I was an infant, I was one of those babies that cried all the time. It was really hard to put me to sleep. People would constantly notice that I was frowning all the time. When I was a kid, I was described as neurotic and introverted. I had a lot of phobias including spiders, bugs, rodents, darkness, and ironically, death. I am still very sensitive to caffeine. Drinking coffee made it impossible to sleep at night. I did not think I was different from everyone else. How was I supposed to know being "normal" felt like? When I turned thirteen, we came to Canada. It was very difficult as a newcomer; I had to face discrimination and prejudice. I could sense that my mental health was getting worse and worse. Someone asked me if my experience was particularly harsh. The answer is no. It was typical as a newcomer, but because I was very sensitive and weak, it would take me forever to get over a negative encounter whereas someone else in the same shoes as I was might not care at all. I remembered between seventeen and eighteen, the year prior to my onset of depression, I would stay awake throughout the entire night for countless nights. Falling asleep was always difficult. I was thinking all the time. The pace of my thoughts was always very fast. I had this enormous amount of mental energy. I also became increasingly negative, always thought of people and things in their worst. When I turned eighteen, I started dating. At the time, it was very special. I was extremely obsessed and manic.

When the relationship ended, that's when the insomnia started and the clinical symptoms of depression began to unfold.

The Big Misconception about Suicides

When I was deeply suicidal, the one question people asked me the most was: why would you kill yourself for someone you dated for only four weeks? They tried to talk me out of my depression by saying, "Oh, get over him," or "This girl got dumped after being with this guy for seven years, she moved on, you should too". People thought that I wanted to die because of love, which in my case was a very petty reason. In fact, when someone just committed suicide, the biggest question is "why", it seems like they need to have a reason to end their life and the reason has to be huge in order to be understandable, such as the death of a child or a bankruptcy. Well, this is a big misconception.

I am pretty sure many of you have felt depressed before. But would you say your depression was caused by situational factors? And once the external problems have been dealt with, you would feel better right away. In such case depression is a *mental state*. It is temporary. It's relatively easy to treat. For some people, they go away on a vacation and come back being happy again. Depression of such nature is like a common cold; our body is able to recover from it spontaneously. On the other hand, depression with a strong genetic predisposition, like the one I have, is a *mental illness*. It's a medical condition; it's *not* a psychological condition by nature—it's a medical condition that produces psychological symptoms. In many cases, it cannot be cured but can only be treated.

There are Many Differences Between the Two Types of Depressions

Trigger of depression. For common depression, people usually have a good reason to be depressed during which a traumatic event took place; whereas for a depression disorder, people do not need to have a reason to commit suicide. Some people would feel suicidal simply because they do not have a healthy lifestyle. They smoke and drink excessively, they lack sleep on a regular basis, and party all the time. If there is a genetic predisposition, their depression will be easily triggered when a trivial obstacle comes their way.

Differences in the severity of symptoms. For common depression, the symptoms are emotional; it has to do with people's feelings being hurt. People want to die, but they have a choice, they could choose to end their life or carry on living. That was the case in my second episode of depression. The reason of my depression was mainly about my physical disability; though the symptoms were severe, I still had control over them, and thankfully, I did not hurt myself again. Whereas for a depression disorder, the symptoms are much more physical and medical in nature, the symptoms are impossible to be conquered by will powers. During my first episode of depression, I didn't just want to die, I need to die. I had no choice. My body was shutting down after not being able to sleep at all for over two months.

Family history. A depression disorder usually has a family history of mental illness, any type of mental illness. In my case, everyone on my father's side is perfectly healthy. They are happy and optimistic people. The person that has a problem is my mom's mom. My maternal grandma suffers from anxiety disorder, her thoughts are always irrational, and she doesn't sleep very much, averagely three or four hours a day. Though my parents are mentally healthy, when my mom was pregnant with me, she was going through a long period of distress because of a family conflict. That might have something to do with it.

Age of onset. Common depression really depends on the onset of a stressor. But for mental illnesses, though it could happen at any age, the typical age of onset of a full-blown episode is between eighteen to twenty-four years old, the ages when hormones are going viral. However, more and more kids as young as eight or nine years old have reported of feeling suicidal. Depression is also prevalent among women who have just given birth or during menopause. It always happens when our body is going through changes. Mental health is part of a person's physical health. When the rest of our body is healthy, we sleep well, eat well, and do exercise, our mental health will also improve.

Treatment. To treat a common depression, a person might be temporarily placed on antidepressant or receive psychotherapy or consulting. For some people "time is the best remedy". Whereas in my case, I personally think that medication is the only effective treatment. Because it is a medical condition, it is not a psychological condition. It's like someone who is born with type 1 diabetes and they have to rely on insulin for life. People like me, we are born with a deficient, and therefore we need to rely on psychotropic medications to restore and maintain our mental health.

Medications—the Right Type and the Right Dosage

Often people with mental illness refuse to take medications or stay on a medication; they think that they are either ineffective or they are doing even more damages. This is actually true. Medications take time to show their result. Often it will take between 21 and 60 days to show the full effect of the medications. Moreover, it is very difficult to find the right type of medication that suits a particular person. The first medication I took had a side effect that made me gain 60lbs by the time I was discharged from the hospital. The second medication I was on gave me severe acne. In 2007, my psychiatrist decided to put me on Epival; it is primarily an anti-seizure medication. Amazingly, I woke up one day and felt like I was different. I couldn't explain in what way, but I was just happier for no reason. I never felt that way in the first twenty-two years of my life. As I took that medication more and more, I realized I finally knew how it feels like to be a "normal" human. My personality changed. I am now a very outgoing and positive person. I don't have phobias anymore, and I sleep like a baby every night. My musical and artistic abilities have also enhanced. I have truly reached my potential as a person and a human being because of this medication.

Though finding the right type of medication is the key in treatment, it is still not enough. The right dosage is equally important. For instance, not every middle-aged female weighing around 160lbs should be prescribed with the same dosage of medication—everyone has a different metabolic rate. It took me about two years of experiment to figure out the right amount of medication for me. There was one time my pharmacy ran out of pills in 125mg. Instead, they gave me pills in 250mg. Without knowing the difference, I mistakenly took twice the usual amount for over a month. During that month, I felt so odd. I became lazy and moody. I didn't want to do exercise, and I was hungry all the time. I gained 15lbs by the end of the month. Then, my mom discovered the mistake. Within a week being back on the right amount of meds, I was myself again. Therefore, it's important to be on the exact amount of medication that's custom to that particular person.

Bipolar Disorder

Many artists, musicians, and scientist have bipolar disorder or other types of mental illness, such as Robin Williams, Demi Lovato, Catherine Zeta-Jones, Vincent van Gogh, John Nash, etc. About three years after my injury, I was finally diagnosed with bipolar disorder. There are many theories as to the cause of this condition. One study found that we are born with up to twenty percent more neurons in our brain compared to an average person; another study found that the neurons of a bipolar patient are particularly excitable. I endorse these two theories. They explain as to why I used to be extremely restless and was always overflowing with mental energy. This is also why an anti-seizure medication works for me. Just like how it is able to lower down the neural activities inside an epileptic patient, it can also calm my over-active brain. However, having this condition is both a curse and a blessing. With that many more excitable neurons in our brain, our imagination, creativity and intelligence are also above average. This is also the reason as to why drug abuse is so prevalent in Hollywood. Many such talented people are suffering from mental illness; therefore, using drugs could be a way of self-medicating.

Why is Mental Illness so Hard to Treat:

It is a very subjective illness. It cannot be detected by blood test, x-ray, MRI, or other methods to diagnose an illness. Even the psychiatrists have a lot of limitations in knowing how each patient feels and what type of illness they actually have. Like me, I was not correctly diagnosed until three years after my injury. Therefore, patients are the only ones who can access their own inner state, but most of them are too sick to even think and too easy to give up. And most importantly, they lack the knowledge and insight to help themselves.

It's hard to find the right type of medication and the right dosage. As mentioned earlier, the side effects of some medications can even worsen the symptoms and make a person even more suicidal. Side effects such as appetite change, weight gain, acne, aloofness, low sex drive, etc. are big deals to most people. They could become the very cause of depression. Therefore, if one medication doesn't work, keep on looking and trying on other types of medication. Do not give up on meds. Do not stop taking meds even if you are feeling better. My condition is treatable, but I don't think it's curable. I'll take my meds unconditionally every day for the rest of my life. I might compromise my chances of having my biological child, but nothing is more important than the quality of my mental health.

The lack of social support is also a big problem for the mentally ill. When you are crazy and lose your mind, you really need someone to take you to a psychiatric facility and act on your behalf. But unfortunately, in many cases, when someone is mentally ill, people walk away from their life when they need social support the most. When a person loses their job, their romantic partner and other meaningful possessions during their acute state, how are they able to feel happy again even if they are biochemically restored?

The Best of Q&As I Have Over the Years

Q: Your injury is preventable, but is your bipolar disorder preventable?

A: I was born with this condition. I think it was almost inevitable that I would become suicidal one day. It would happen sooner or later. However, if I knew enough about my condition since day one, I would probably start taking medications at an earlier age. For instance, if I started treatment at the age of 16, I probably would not have had a full-blown episode.

Q: What would happen if you stop taking medications?

A: If I skip a dosage, I would probably know right away as the pace of my thoughts will pick up at night and I'd be unable to fall asleep. Without a night of sleep, my heart would beat faster and I would be a little bit more emotional and neurotic the next day. Therefore, I make sure that I take my meds unconditionally every day and when I travel, I pack them in two different suitcases just in case one of them goes missing. I have developed a dependency on my medications, perhaps you can compare that to an addict who cannot live without their drugs. However, I would define mine as healthy.

Just like someone who is born with type 1 diabetes, they need to rely on insulin for the rest of their life. Having a bipolar disorder is innate and I need to rely on something extra to keep me balanced and functional. But unlike someone who has diabetes, they have to watch what they eat and change their lifestyle accordingly, when I stay on my medications, my life is perfectly normal.

Q: If my loved one is depressed and suicidal, what should I do for them?

A: Take them to a psychiatric facility to prevent this person from hurting themselves and other people. I have heard so many stories of family members trying so hard to prevent their child from committing suicide. They take turns to watch the person to a point where everyone is extremely exhausted. At the end, they still could not prevent tragedies from happening. Locking a person in a psychiatric facility is the safest thing. All of those psychotropic medications take at least three weeks to kick in. During this important period, a person has to be monitored to prevent self-inflicted harm. The condition of a psychiatric facility in a developed country like Canada and the United States might not be as comfortable as a hotel, but it is really not that bad.

Q: Did culture play a role in your case and how you initially perceive your condition?

A: Yes, maybe. Growing up, I have never heard about depression or bipolar disorder. Thirteen years ago, there was very little awareness campaign on mental health issues. I didn't think I was medically ill. I thought and everyone around me thought I was suicidal because my boyfriend dumped me. Therefore, it was shameful to reach out for help and even when I did, people were judgemental and made things worse. From TV or movies, mentally ill people were always portrayed as scary and incurable; psychiatric facilities were like zoos or concentration camps. It was more so growing up in an Asian culture. Therefore, I really resisted of going to a psychiatric facility. I did not think it would be helpful, which was a huge mistake. After my injury,

I was in and out of psychiatry for a total of six months. In actuality, it is the most ideal environment for recovery.

Q: Did you seek for professional help during your acute stage? And are they helpful?

A: I was seen by one social worker, one family doctor, and two psychiatrists before my injury. They were not very helpful. The social worker and the family doctor were not specially trained in severe psychiatric conditions. Again, like everyone else, they were trying to talk me out of my depression. They failed to understand that my condition is a medical problem. As to the two psychiatrists, one of them wrote me a note saying I am not mentally capable of completing my high school exams. The other psychiatrist prescribed me with anti-depressant and discharged me back to the community after three days I overdosed myself with sleeping pills. I felt like they could have explained to me what was really going on and gave me more assurance that this was a treatable condition. When the anti-depressant didn't start working right away, I quickly lost faith on the meds, and lost faith on doctors as a whole, thinking if they could not even help me, who could? I thought I would remain crazy for the rest of my life and that was my last straw. After my injury, I saw my psychiatrist Dr. McCullagh for the first time. He was my doctor for the next ten years. Right away, he was different from others. He was compassionate. Had I met someone like him prior to my injury, I wonder if it would have made the difference. Therefore, if you are discouraged by a health care professional, look for another one and keep on looking for someone who can truly help. I think a good doctor should have the heart of a parent, when they treat their patients as if they are their child, not only they are a good doctor, they are a great human being.

Q: Tell us about some of the myth and fact about people who committed suicide?

A: In general, women are more likely to report of feeling suicidal because gender role allows women to be vulnerable. Women tend to choose methods that are less lethal during their initial attempt, such as taking sleeping pills or slitting their wrist. They sometimes do that as a way of getting people's attention and console. They want people to know that they are serious about wanting to commit suicide and they need help from them. At the back of their mind, they want to be saved. On the other hand, men are less likely to disclose their suicidal thoughts for the fear of being judged. Without being able to talk about their problems, their negative emotions could quickly become intense. They are more likely to choose methods that are more lethal, such as jumping off a subway track or shot themselves. They want to make sure that they could successfully die. They won't risk the humiliation of having a failed attempt. As I wrote in my memoir, after one month without sleep, I was deeply suicidal. Though I wanted to die so bad, I was still afraid about all the pain and suffering before death. That's because fearing for death is a human nature. Therefore, I chose to over-dosage myself on sleeping pills. It was an easy way out. But after two months without sleep, I completely lost my humanity. I'd do anything to die. I no longer cared about how to die.

Q: Did you think of hurting an innocent person? What do you think of the school shootings in the U.S. perpetrated by people who are mentally ill?

A: Yes, I did attempt to kill my dad. At that time, I was incapable of feeling love and sympathy. The illness turned me into a sociopath, literally. My nature and the basic elements of my humanity were taken away by my illness. I'd do anything to kill myself and because my parents were protecting me, I was about to kill them as well. This explains why we hear stories of mother killing their own children when they have depression.

As to the second question. I can't understand their action, but I can definitely relate to their mentality. When a person is at the end of their rope, they'd feel jealous of people who are better off than they are. That's why those incidences always take place in a school, they seldom happen in a nursing home. Secondly, killing one's self is a huge commitment. It takes a lot of guts to do it. By committing a horrible crime, they basically leave themselves with no choice but to kill themselves, better yet, the police could do the job for them. Again, a mental illness can strip a person of their humanity. I don't think all of them are pure evil. They are sick and they don't believe that they are treatable. If gun control is not possible, then extensive levels of education on mental illness might be the solution to prevent more tragedies from happening.

Q: Describe the role of faith on your journey?

A: Medication will only bring me to the level of an average person. But I feel like my mental health is better than an average person. Over the years, I have experienced things that are incredibly harsh and disheartening. I still live with chronic pain every day. My body and physical ability will only decline as I age more. Yet I have joy, peace, and hope beyond understanding. God's words really made a huge impact on how I handled the people and the situation in my life. He taught me to forgive and give grace. He made me see the silver lining behind every obstacle. When bad thing happens, I just tell myself that there is a good reason behind it, and I will endure to find out what. I believe that He saved me on that day for a higher purpose, and I am already living it. I was too proud to become a Christian by just listening to someone's preaching. I believed in Him because I personally experienced His presence and intervention. I would take the same miserable path all over again if that was the only way leading me to Jesus.

Final Messages

The stigma against mentally ill people is still prevalent. By mentally ill, I don't just mean the ones who are obviously insane and psychotic. Sometimes, I feel like I am still being judged because of my mental health history. Everyone in this world has a different threshold as to how much stress they can take before a psychological meltdown. The same stressful event that happens on you might mean nothing to you, but it could mean a great deal to someone else. A person's capacity to handle stressors is predetermined by genetics. It's not something that they have power over. They cannot just "tough it up" or "snap out of it". A mental illness is an illness of our brain, the largest and most complicated organ in our body. If every single part of our body is allowed to get sick, then why is it that an illness of our brain is stigmatized? It's those stigmas that prevent a person from seeking for help and receiving the proper help. We need to do more as a society in treating people with mental illness. Patients suffer long waiting periods in emergency and are often set low on the priority list because they show no physical wounds. They need to have more access to counseling and medications without financial barriers.

My message for suicide survivors: I have read many stories written by people who have lost someone due to suicide. They blame themselves for not being able to do enough to save their loved ones. My parents did everything humanly possible to protect and save me, yet it still happened. Looking back, it was almost impossible to prevent me from making that ultimate attempt. I was just really blessed that I still had the use of my brain and my upper body. My point is, it's an illness that is as severe as a terminal illness. It's akin to losing someone due to cancer. It's not your fault, especially if you have done all you could to help. If you believe in heaven, believe that you will meet again one day.

Lastly, a message for people who are going through tough times: There were countless days when I thought my world had ended. Fortunately, I endured and was able to see the day of my salvation. There is nothing in this world that you cannot get over with. I can guarantee that most of you will never be as messed up as I once was. If you feel like ending your life is the only solution, then that means you are sick, medically sick. You need to seek for treatment. It might take a while, took me more than four years, but eventually it will be overcome. At the end of the journey, what doesn't kill you makes you stronger. You might even realize it's a blessing in disguise.

Thank you for reading this book, and please share.
Like Leap on Facebook
Find me on Twitter: @xianancy315

Visit my blog where I write about stories that make you smile:
www.elevensummers.blogspot.ca

Thank you tons!

ACKNOWLEDGEMENTS

I want to thank Harley Nott, Paul Britton and Brad
Clark for editing and proof-reading my manu-
script. Your time and effort is greatly appreciated!

I want to thank everyone who encouraged me to share my story.

To my church family and my dear friends, thank you
for always supporting me and praying for me.

To Mom and Dad, thank you for raising me, suffering for me and loving me always and forever.

To everyone who came to my life and made it better, thank you.